M

W9-AWR-929

GREAT WRITING 4

Great Essays

FOURTH EDITION

KEITH S. FOLSE
UNIVERSITY OF CENTRAL FLORIDA

APRIL MUCHMORE-VOKOUN
HILLSBOROUGH COMMUNITY COLLEGE

ELENA VESTRI SOLOMON
KHALIFA UNIVERSITY OF SCIENCE, TECHNOLOGY,
AND RESEARCH, UAE

**NATIONAL
GEOGRAPHIC
LEARNING**
|

**CENGAGE
Learning**

Australia • Brazil • Japan • Korea • Mexico • Singapore • Spain • United Kingdom • United States

Great Writing 4: Great Essays
Fourth Edition
Keith S. Folse, April Muchmore-Vokoun, Elena
Vestri Solomon

Publisher: Sherrise Roehr

Executive Editor: Laura Le Dréan

Development Editors: Katherine Carroll,
Charlotte Sturdy

Director of Global Marketing: Ian Martin

Senior Product Marketing Manger:
Emily Stewart

International Marketing Manager:
Caitlin Thomas

Director of Content and Media Production:
Michael Burggren

Senior Content Project Manager: Daisy Sosa

Senior Print Buyer: Mary Beth Hennebury

Cover Design: Christopher Roy and
Michael Rosenquest

Cover Image: MATT RAMBO/National
Geographic Stock

Interior Design: Aysling Design

Composition: PreMediaGlobal, Inc.

U.S. Edition

ISBN-13: 978-1-285-19494-3

International Student Edition

ISBN-13: 978-1-285-75062-0

National Geographic Learning/Cengage Learning
20 Channel Center Street
Boston, MA 02210
USA

Cengage Learning is a leading provider of customized learning solutions with office locations around the globe, including Singapore, the United Kingdom, Australia, Mexico, Brazil, and Japan.

Cengage Learning products are represented in Canada by Nelson Education, Ltd.

Visit National Geographic Learning online at **ngl.cengage.com**

Visit our corporate website at **www.cengage.com**

Printed in the United States of America
4 5 6 7 18 17 16

Contents

Scope and Sequence

Unit	Writing	Grammar for Writing	Building Better Vocabulary	Original Student Writing
1 p. 2 **EXPLORING THE ESSAY**	• What is an Essay? • Example Essays • Writing the Introduction • Writing the Body • Writing the Conclusion		• Word Associations • Using Collocations	**Original Student Writing:** Write an Essay **Photo Topic:** Describe a festival or celebration in your culture. **Timed Writing Topic:** What are the benefits of knowing a second language?
2 p. 38 **NARRATIVE ESSAYS**	• What is a Narrative Essay? • Example Narrative Essays • Developing a Narrative Essay	• Connectors and Time Relationship Words • Sentence Variety with Prepositions of Time Plus Key Nouns for Better Cohesion • Adjective Clauses	• Word Associations • Using Collocations	**Original Student Writing:** Write a Narrative Essay **Photo Topic:** Write a story about a person who inspires you. **Timed Writing Topic:** Narrate a story about a disagreement you had with a friend (or family member) and how the disagreement was resolved.
3 p. 64 **COMPARISON ESSAYS**	• What is a Comparison Essay? • Example Comparison Essays • Developing a Comparison Essay • Developing Ideas for Writing	• Sentence Structure of Connectors (for Comparison Essays) • Connectors That Show Comparison Between Sentences of Paragraphs • Connectors That Show Contrast Between Sentences of Paragraphs • Using Adverb Clauses	• Word Associations • Using Collocations	**Original Student Writing:** Write a Comparison Essay **Photo Topic:** Compare or contrast two places on Earth. **Timed Writing Topic:** Compare two popular vacation destinations

Unit	Writing	Grammar for Writing	Building Better Vocabulary	Original Student Writing
4 p. 88 **CAUSE-EFFECT ESSAYS**	• What Is a Cause-Effect Essay? • Example Cause-Effect Essays • Developing a Cause-Effect Essay • Choosing Words Carefully • Developing Ideas for Writing	• Connectors for Cause-Effect Essays • Connectors That Show Cause • Connectors That Show Effect • Noun Clauses	• Word Associations • Using Collocations	**Original Student Writing:** Write a Cause-Effect Essay **Photo Topic:** Write about some effects of extreme weather. **Timed Writing Topic:** Why do people keep pets?
5 p. 112 **ARGUMENT ESSAYS**	• What Is an Argument Essay? • Example Argument Essay • Developing an Argument Essay	• Controlling Tone with Modals • Using the *if* clause	• Word Associations • Using Collocations	**Original Student Writing:** Write an Argument Essay **Photo Topic:** Write an argument essay about industry vs. nature. **Timed Writing Topic:** What should happen to students who are caught cheating on an exam? Why?
6 p. 136 **OTHER FORMS OF ACADEMIC WRITING**	• Part I: What Is a Reaction/ Response Essay? • Example Reaction Essay • Part II: Understanding Written Exam or Essay Questions	• Understanding Sentence Types	• Word Associations • Using Collocations	**Original Student Writing:** Write a Reaction/ Response Essay **Photo Topic:** Write a response essay that describes your emotion and reaction to a photograph. **Timed Writing Topics:** Question 1: Summarize the main points of this textbook. Question 2: Evaluate your own academic writing skills.

Overview

Framed by engaging **National Geographic** images, the new edition of the *Great Writing* series helps students write better sentences, paragraphs, and essays. The new *Foundations* level meets the needs of low-level learners through practice in basic grammar, vocabulary, and spelling, while all levels feature clear explanations, student writing models, and meaningful practice opportunities. The new edition of the *Great Writing* series is perfect for beginning to advanced learners, helping them develop and master academic writing skills.

Great Writing: Foundations focuses on basic sentence construction, emphasizing grammar, vocabulary, spelling, and composition.

Great Writing 1 focuses on sentences as they appear in paragraphs.

Great Writing 2 teaches paragraph development.

Great Writing 3 transitions from paragraphs to essays.

Great Writing 4 focuses on essays.

Great Writing 5 practices more advanced essays.

The earliest ESL composition textbooks were merely extensions of ESL grammar classes. The activities in these books did not practice English composition as much as ESL grammar points. Later books, on the other hand, tended to focus too much on the composing process. We feel that this focus ignores the important fact that the real goal for English learners is both to produce a presentable product and to understand the composing process. From our years of ESL and other L2 teaching experience, we believe that the *Great Writing* series allows English learners to achieve this goal.

Great Writing 4: Great Essays provides introductory instruction and extensive practical exercises and activities in essay writing at the high-intermediate and advanced levels. This book contains a wide variety of exercises that offer practice in both working with the writing process and developing a final written product. We assume that students can write good paragraphs and that what they need is instruction in, modeling of, and guidance with essays.

This book is designed for high-intermediate to advanced students. Depending on the class level and the amount of writing that is done outside of class hours, there is enough material for 60 to 80 classroom hours. Provided that enough writing is done outside of the classroom, the number of hours can be as little as 40.

Organization

In *Great Writing 4*, Units 1–6 deal with the elements of a good essay. Unit 1 presents the overall organization of an essay, and offers some specific suggestions for writing the introduction of an essay, including how to write a good hook and a solid thesis statement. Units 2 through 6 teach five different kinds of essays—narrative, comparison, cause-effect, argument, and reaction. While it is not necessary to cover these five essay types in the given order, the current sequencing will allow for some recycling of grammatical and lexical items. The *Brief Writer's Handbook with Activities* and the Appendices contain additional practice material to support both the process and the mechanics of writing.

Contents of a Unit

Although each unit has specific writing objectives (listed at the beginning of the unit), the following features appear in every unit:

Example Essays

Because we believe that writing and reading are inextricably related, the 22 example essays model a rhetorical mode and/or provide editing activities. Many models are preceded by schema-building questions and followed by questions about organization, syntactic structures, or other composition features. New, potentially unfamiliar vocabulary words are glossed at the end of each paragraph. These words can provide students with a list of vocabulary to add to a separate vocabulary notebook.

Grammar for Writing

Since good writing requires a working knowledge of the mechanics of English, *Great Writing 4* includes clear charts and detailed instruction that relates directly to the writing assignments. In addition, numerous activities give students the opportunity to practice and refine their grammar and writing knowledge and skills.

Activities

The new fourth edition contains numerous activities, suggestions for additional essay writing assignments, and supplemental activities in The *Brief Writer's Handbook*. These writing, grammar, and vocabulary activities gradually build the skills students need to write well-crafted essays and provide learners with more input in English composition and paragraph organization and cohesion. To this end, the activities in this book deal with elements that affect the quality of a written product, including grammar, organization, and logic. Although in this text there is information about both process and product in essay writing, it should be noted that the focus is slightly more on the final written product.

Building Better Vocabulary

Each unit includes two vocabulary activities to build schema and collocations. In the first activity, Word Associations, the students identify words that best relate to the target vocabulary word. This allows them to build connections to more words and thus grow their vocabulary more quickly. Words from the Academic Word List are starred (see pages 183–184 for the complete list). The second activity, Using Collocations, helps students learn specific word combinations, or collocations, which will improve their writing. It is helpful to encourage students to use these new words in their Original Student Writing assignment and to add them to a vocabulary notebook.

Writer's Notes

Great Writing 4 features writing advice that helps writers to better understand use and format.

Building Better Sentences

Periodically in each unit, students are asked to turn to Appendix 1 and work on building better sentences. Each practice is intentionally short and includes only three problems. In each problem, there are three to five short sentences that the students must combine into a single sentence that expresses all the ideas in a logical and grammatically correct manner.

Original Student Writing

Each unit includes an activity that requires students to do some form of writing. Original Student Writing includes writing prompts and a set of directions to encourage students to follow the writing process and refer back to the lessons taught in the unit.

Additional Writing Topics gives students the opportunity to continue practicing their writing skills. The first topic always links back to the opening photograph and writing prompt. The instructor can decide whether all students will write about the same topic or whether each student is free to choose any of the topics listed.

Peer Editing

At the end of each unit, a peer editing activity offers students the opportunity to provide written comments to one another with the goal of improving their essays. Peer editing sheets for each unit can be found at NGL.Cengage.com/GW4 and provide the guidance and structure necessary for students at this level to perform this task successfully. There is also a sample in Appendix 2 on page 208. We recommend that students spend 15 to 20 minutes reading a classmate's essay and writing comments using the questions on the peer editing sheet.

Timed Writing

One way to improve students' comfort level with the task of writing under a deadline, such as during a testing situation, is to provide them with numerous writing opportunities that are timed. The final activity in each unit features a timed-writing prompt geared toward the grammar and sentence structure presented in that unit. Students are given five minutes to read the prompt and make a quick writing plan, followed by 40 minutes of actual writing. Instructors may use this activity at any time during the lesson.

What's New in This Edition?

- Engaging images from *National Geographic* connect learning to the greater world.

- New and updated essays act as springboards and models for writing.

- Updated Grammar for Writing sections clearly present grammar and help students learn the structures for writing.

- Streamlined instruction and practice activities offer step-by-step guidelines to focus writers on both the writing process and product.

- Words from the Academic Word List are highlighted in vocabulary activities, encouraging students to expand their word knowledge.

- The expanded *Brief Writer's Handbook with Activities* now includes a Useful Vocabulary for Better Writing section to help writers choose appropriate language for the different rhetorical modes.

- An all-new level, *Great Writing: Foundations* introduces students to the basics of grammar, spelling, and vocabulary.

- A new unit addresses additional writing assignments students may encounter, further preparing them for the types of writing tasks they will have in college.

- A new Online Workbook encourages learners to further practice grammar, vocabulary, and editing skills. Students can also write paragraphs or essays, and submit them to the instructor electronically.

- An updated Presentation Tool allows instructors to use the book in an interactive whiteboard setting and demonstrate the editing process.

- An e-book provides another option to use *Great Writing* in a traditional or blended learning environment.

Ancillary Components

In addition to the *Great Writing 4: Great Essays* Student Book, the following components help both the instructor and the students expand their teaching and learning.

- **Online Workbook:** Includes a wealth of vocabulary, grammar, writing, and editing practice with immediate feedback.

- **Presentation Tool CD-ROM:** Offers instructors the ability to lead whole-class presentations and demonstrate the editing process.

- **Assessment CD-ROM with ExamView®:** Allows instructors to create and customize tests.

- **Teacher Companion Site at NGL.Cengage.com/GW4:** Provides teachers with answer keys, peer editing sheets, and teacher's notes.

- **Student Companion Site at NGL.Cengage.com/GW4:** Provides students with peer editing sheets, glossary, and interactive flashcards.

- **eBook:** Offers an interactive option.

Inside a Unit

Framed by engaging **National Geographic** images, the new edition of the *Great Writing* series helps students write better sentences, paragraphs, and essays. The new *Foundations* level meets the needs of low-level learners through practice in basic grammar vocabulary, and spelling, while all levels feature clear explanations student writing models and meaningful practice opportunities. The new edition of the *Great Writing* series is perfect for beginning to advanced learners, helping them develop and master academic writing skills.

Impactful **National Geographic** images provide an engaging foundation for student writing.

22 Sample Writing Models focus on specific writing skills and rhetorical modes.

Vocabulary words are glossed to encourage independent mastery of new terms.

x

4 _____ I heard him call my name. I ran to the room we shared, sat down on the bed, and watched Claudio close his suitcase. He turned to me and nodded. "It's time, brother," he said. I thought he was referring to his time to leave the house. Actually, he went on to explain all of the important responsibilities that I would have after he was gone. Claudio meant that it was time for me to **take** on a bigger role in the family. _____ that point, I understood everything.

to take on: undertake, face

5 _____ then on, I took my **role** as the "man of the house" very seriously. With Claudio away, I would need to be available for Mom whenever she needed me. What have I learned from my brother? I have learned about family, love, and responsibility.

a role: job, function

Building Better Sentences: For further practice, go to Practice 10 on page 197 In Appendix 1.

Grammar for Writing

Adjective Clauses

Adjective clauses are one of the most powerful ways to combine two ideas (simple sentences) into one complex sentence. Study the following rules and examples:

1. Adjective clauses must contain a subject and a verb.

2. The subject of an adjective clause can be *who* (people), *which* (things), or *that* (people or things).

Samir studies at a university. The university is well known for its technology programs.

adjective clause
Samir studies at a university that is well known for its technology programs.

3. If the information in the adjective clause is necessary to clarify the person or thing you are writing about, do not use a comma to separate the ideas. However, if the information in the adjective clause is not necessary to understand the meaning of the sentence, use a comma, or pair of commas, to separate the adjective clause from the rest of the sentence. In other words, commas indicate the information is extra. Study the examples below.

Necessary Information	Unnecessary Information
The city **that we will visit last on our trip** is located in central Florida.	Orlando, **which we will visit last on our trip**, is located in central Florida.
NOTE: When the writer says *the city*, it is not clear which city the writer is talking about. The adjective clause *(that we will visit last on our trip)* is important information for readers because it tells them which city in central Florida the writer is referring to.	**NOTE:** When the writer says *Orlando*, the readers know which city the writer is talking about. The information about when the writer will visit this city does not affect our ability to know that the writer is referring to Orlando.

Grammar for Writing

New **Grammar for Writing** charts provide clear explanations and examples, giving learners easy access to the structures they will use in their writing.

Building Better Vocabulary

Building Better Vocabulary highlights words from the Academic Word List and helps students to apply and expand their vocabulary and knowledge of important collocations.

Building Better Vocabulary

ACTIVITY 5 Word Associations

Circle the word or phrase that is most closely related to the word or phrase on the left. If necessary, use a dictionary to check the meaning of words you do not know.

	A	B
1. diversity*	difference	distance
2. customs	shirts	traditions
3. a concept*	an idea	a traditional song
4. remarkable	amazing	repetitive

Original Student Writing: Argument Essay

Brainstorming

Brainstorming will help you get started with your argument essay. In this section, you will choose any method of brainstorming that works for you and develop supporting information.

ACTIVITY 11 Choosing a Topic

Follow the steps below to develop ideas for an argument essay.

1. First, choose a thesis statement from the statements that you wrote in Activity 4 on pages 122–123 or choose any other topic and thesis statement that you want to write about. Remember that the topic must have more than one point of view to qualify as an argument.

Essay topic: _____

Thesis statement: _____

Original Student Writing

Original Student Writing gives students the chance to combine the grammar, vocabulary, and writing skills together in one writing piece.

Peer Editing activities increase awareness of common errors and help students become better writers and editors.

Timed Writing prepares students for success on standardized and high-stakes writing exams.

Timed Writing

How quickly can you write in English? There are many times when you must write quickly, such as on a test. It is important to feel comfortable during those times. Timed-writing practice can make you feel better about writing quickly in English.

1. Take out a piece of paper.
2. Read the essay guidelines and the writing prompt.
3. Write a basic outline, including the thesis and your three main points.
4. Write a five-paragraph essay.
5. You have 40 minutes to write your essay.

Narrative Essay Guidelines

- Remember to give your essay a title.
- Double-space your essay.
- Write as legibly as possible (if you are not using a computer).
- Select an appropriate principle of organization for your topic.
- Include a short introduction that serves as background information, three body paragraphs that tell the narrative, and an appropriate conclusion.
- Try to give yourself a few minutes before the end of the activity to review your work. Check for spelling, verb tense, and subject-verb agreement mistakes.

Narrate a story about a disagreement you had with a friend (or family member) and how the disagreement was resolved.

For more practice with the grammar, vocabulary, and writing found in this unit, go to NGL.Cengage.com/GW4.

Technology   *Great Writing 4: Great Essays*

For Instructors:

Assessment CD-ROM with ExamView® allows instructors to create and customize tests and quizzes easily.

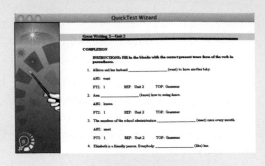

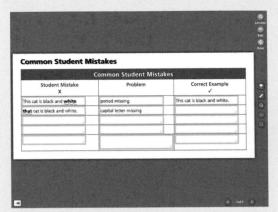

The Presentation Tool CD-ROM contains time-saving, interactive activities from the student book, a set of whiteboard tools, and additional content to help the instructor guide learners through the editing process.

Teacher's Notes, Answer Keys, and Peer Editing Sheets are available online for instructors.

For Students:

Online Workbook: Powered by MyELT, this independent student resource features instructor-led and self-study options and includes additional vocabulary, grammar, writing, and editing practice with immediate feedback.

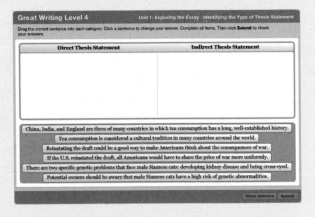

***Great Writing* eBooks** are available for all levels and are compatible with tablets, laptops, and smartphones.

Acknowledgements

We would like to thank the hundreds of ESL and English composition colleagues who have generously shared their ideas, insights, and feedback on second language writing, university English course requirements, and textbook design.

We would also like to thank Laura LeDréan, Thomas Jefferies, Ian Martin, and Emily Stewart for their guidance. We are extremely grateful for the support given to us by our developmental editors Katherine Carroll, Charlotte Sturdy, and Yeny Kim. We also remain forever grateful to our previous editors at Houghton Mifflin: Susan Maguire, Kathy Sands-Boehmer, and Kathleen Smith, for their indispensable guidance throughout the birth and growth of this writing project.

As well, we are indebted to the following reviewers who offered ideas and suggestions that shaped our revisions:

Laura Taylor, Iowa State University, Iowa
Mary Barratt, Iowa State University, Iowa
Abdelhay Belfakir, University of Central Florida, Florida
Taoufik Ferjani, Zayed University, United Arab Emirates
Cheryl Alcorn, Pasadena City College, California
Paul McGarry, Santa Barbara City College, California
Fernanda Ortiz, University of Arizona, Arizona
Michelle Jeffries, University of Arkansas—Fayetteville, Arkansas
Suzanne Medina, California State University—Dominguez Hills, California
Kristi Miller, American English Institute, California
Kevin Van Houten, Glendale Community College, California
Izabella Kojic-Sabo, University of Windsor, Canada
Wayne Fong, Aston School, China
Yiwei Shu, New Oriental School, China
Raul Billini, John F. Kennedy Institute of Languages, Dominican Republic
Rosa Vasquez, John F. Kennedy Institute of Languages, Dominican Republic
Mike Sfiropoulos, Palm Beach State College, Florida
Louise Gobron, Georgia State University, Georgia
Gabriella Cambiasso, City College of Chicago—Harold Washington, Illinois
Lin Cui, Harper College, Illinois
Laura Aoki, Kurume University, Japan
Rieko Ashida, Konan University, Japan
Greg Holloway, Kyushu Institute of Technology, Japan
Collin James, Kansai Gaigo University, Japan
Lindsay Mack, Ritsumeikan Asia Pacific University, Japan
Robert Staehlin, Morioka University, Japan
Jenny Selvidge, Donnelly College, Kansas
Phan Vongphrachanh, Donnelly College, Kansas
Virginia Van Hest Bastaki, Kuwait University, Kuwait
Jennifer Jakubic, Century College, Minnesota
Trina Goslin, University of Nevada—Reno, Nevada
Margaret Layton, University of Nevada—Reno, Nevada
Amy Metcalf, University of Nevada—Reno, Nevada
Gail Fernandez, Bergen Community College, New Jersey
Lynn Meng, Union County College—Elizabeth, New Jersey

Zoe Isaacson, Queens College, New York

Sherwin Kizner, Queens College, New York

Linnea Spitzer, Portland State University, Oregon

Jennifer Stenseth, Portland State University, Oregon

Rebecca Valdovinos, Oregon State University, Oregon

Renata Ruff, Prince Mohammed University, Saudi Arabia

Ya Li Chao, National Taichung University of Science and Technology, Taiwan

Kuei-ping Hsu, National Tsing Hua University, Taiwan

Morris Huang, National Taiwan University of Science and Technology, Taiwan

Cheng-Che Lin, Tainan University of Technology, Taiwan

Rita Yeh, Chia Nan University of Pharmacy and Science, Taiwan

Nguyen Chanh Tri, Vietnam Australia International School, Vietnam

Mai Minh Tien, Vietnam Australia International School, Vietnam

Tuan Nguyen, Vietnam Australia International School, Vietnam

Nguyen Thi Thanh The, Vietnam Australia International School, Vietnam

Nguyen Vu Minh Phuong, Vietnam Australia International School, Vietnam

Colleen Comidy, Seattle Central Community College, Washington

Cindy Etter, University of Washington, Washington

Kris Hardy, Seattle Central Community College, Washington

Liese Rajesh, Seattle Central Community College, Washington

Finally, many thanks go to our students who have taught us what ESL composition ought to be. Without them, this work would have been impossible.

Keith S. Folse
April Muchmore-Vokoun
Elena Vestri Solomon

Photo Credits

Traditional Castellers build a human castle during La Merce Festival in Barcelona, Spain.

Can you describe a festival or celebration in your culture?

What Is an Essay?

An essay is a short collection of paragraphs that presents facts, opinions, and ideas about a topic. Topics can range from a description of a visit to the beach to a hike in the Himalayas to an argument for or against nuclear energy.

Kinds of Essays

There are many different ways to write an essay. The method that a writer chooses is often determined by the topic of the essay. The writer needs to consider what kind of essay will convey his or her ideas in the clearest and most accurate way. This book contains examples of five common kinds of essays: **narrative**, **comparison**, **cause-effect**, **argument**, and **reaction**. Each of the next five units presents one of these rhetorical styles of essay writing.

It is very rare for anyone to write an essay that is exclusively one style. Most writers use more than one method within the same essay. For example, if you are comparing the lifestyles of actors and professional athletes, you might include information about how actors and professional athletes got their start in their careers (cause-effect). You might also give an account of a specific athlete's story (narrative). In addition, your essay could include facts and opinions about how one profession is more respected than the other (comparison and argument). Once you learn about these essay methods separately and become comfortable with them, you can experiment with weaving them together to produce well-written essays in English.

Parts of an Essay

An essay has three basic parts: the **introduction**, the **body**, and the **conclusion**. The introduction is the first paragraph, the conclusion is the last paragraph, and the body consists of the paragraph or paragraphs in between. The most basic and versatile format for an essay consists of five paragraphs. In a typical five-paragraph essay, paragraph one introduces the topic, paragraphs two through four develop the topic by giving details, and paragraph five concludes the essay.

```
┌──────────────────┐
│   Introduction   │
└──────────────────┘

┌──────────────────┐
│ Body Paragraph 1 │
└──────────────────┘

┌──────────────────┐
│ Body Paragraph 2 │
└──────────────────┘

┌──────────────────┐
│ Body Paragraph 3 │
└──────────────────┘

┌──────────────────┐
│    Conclusion    │
└──────────────────┘
```

The first paragraph, or introduction, introduces the topic to the reader and includes the **thesis statement**. The thesis states the main idea of the essay and tells what the organization of the information will be. This paragraph usually begins with a hook. The hook is one or more sentences that get the reader's attention. A hook can be a famous quote, a broad statement, a question, a statistic, an anecdote or short story, or an interesting piece of information.

Each paragraph in the **body** of the essay includes a **topic sentence** and **supporting sentences**. The topic sentence tells the reader the main topic of the paragraph. Sometimes it also gives the reader information about the writer's purpose. Supporting sentences relate to the topic sentence of the paragraph in which they occur. Common supporting sentences give examples, reasons, facts, or more specific information about the topic. Without supporting sentences, an essay would be nothing more than a general outline.

Finally, it is important for an essay to have a good **conclusion**. The introduction and the conclusion often share some of the same ideas and words in order to remind the reader of the main idea of the essay. Conclusions often present suggestions, predictions, or opinions related to the topic.

ACTIVITY 1 Studying a Classification Essay

This is a classification essay about household chores. Discuss the Preview Questions with a classmate. Then read the essay and answer the questions that follow.

Preview Questions

1. How much time do you spend cleaning your house or apartment each week?

2. What is your least favorite household chore? Why?

General Topic
عام شي موضوع كامل واسع دايله

Cinderella and Her <u>Tedious</u> Household Chores

tedious: boring;
monotonous

1   Almost everyone knows how the story of Cinderella ends, but do people actually think about how she spent her days before she met the prince? Her daily routine was not glamorous. She did everything from sweeping the floors to cooking the meals. If someone had asked Cinderella which chores she did not particularly like, she probably would have answered, "Why, none, of course. Housework is my duty!" In today's increasingly busy society, however, most people admit that they have definite dislikes for certain household chores. The top three of these unpopular tasks often include ironing clothes, washing dishes, and cleaning the bathroom.

Topic

2   One of the most hated chores for many people is ironing clothes. It is not a task that can be completed quickly or thoughtlessly. Each piece of clothing must be handled individually, so ironing a basket of laundry can take hours! After ironing a piece of clothing **meticulously**, which **entails** smoothing out the fabric, following the seams, and getting the creases just right, it needs to be put on a hanger as soon as possible. If not, this item might become **wrinkled** and need to be ironed again. Perhaps the reason that ironing is not a favorite chore is that it requires extreme attention to detail from beginning to end.

meticulously:
  thoroughly and very
  carefully

to entail: to include

wrinkled: having an
  unwanted line or
  crease; not ironed

3   Another household chore that many people dislike is washing dishes. Of course, some people claim that this chore is no longer a problem because dishwashers are available now! However, no one would argue that dishes, **silverware**, and especially pots and pans

silverware: eating
  utensils, such as
  forks, knives, and
  spoons

washed in a dishwasher come out as clean as they do when washed by hand. For this reason, many people continue to wash their dishes by hand, but they are not necessarily happy doing it. Washing dishes is a dirty job that requires not only **elbow grease** to scrub food off the dishes but also patience to rinse and dry them. In addition, unlike ironing clothes, washing dishes is a chore that usually must be done every day. Regardless of how Cinderella felt about this particular chore, it is obvious that most people do not enjoy doing it.

elbow grease: physical strength, usually using the hands

4   Although ironing clothes and washing dishes are not the most pleasant household chores, perhaps the most **dreaded** chore is cleaning the bathroom. This task involves **tackling** three main areas: the bathtub, sink, and toilet. Because the bathroom is full of germs, a quick wiping of the surfaces is often not enough. As a result, strong bathroom cleansers are necessary to clean and **disinfect** this room. The task of cleaning the bathroom is so unpleasant that some people wear rubber gloves when they attempt it. The only positive point about cleaning the bathroom is that it does not have to be done on a daily basis.

dreaded: feared

to tackle: to undertake, begin

to disinfect: to purify, eliminate germs

5   Maintaining a house means doing a wide variety of unpleasant chores. Cinderella knew this, and so does the rest of the world. Many individuals do not have the luxury of hiring an outside person to do their housework, so they must **make do** with their own resources. Still, taking pride in the results of this hard work helps many people get through the unpleasantness of these chores.

to make do: to manage with what is available

Post-Reading

1. In a few words, describe the hook of this essay. _____

_____   _____

2. Do you think this hook is effective? Does it grab your attention? Why or why not?

_____

_____

3. According to the author of this essay, what are the three least popular household chores?

_____   _____   _____

4. How many paragraphs does this essay have? _____ Which paragraph is the introduction? _____ Which paragraph is the conclusion? _____ Which paragraphs make up the body? _____

5. What is the general topic of this essay? _____

_____

6. Can you find a sentence in Paragraph 1 that tells readers what to expect in Paragraphs 2, 3, and 4? Write that sentence here. _____

_____

7. What topic is discussed in Paragraph 2? _____

_____

8. Write the topic sentences of Paragraphs 3 and 4.

Paragraph 3: _____

_____

_____

Paragraph 4: _____

_____

_____

9. In Paragraph 2, the writer shows that people do not like to iron clothes. Write two of the supporting sentences here.

_____

_____

_____

_____

10. In Paragraph 4, the writer suggests that cleaning the bathroom is not a fast chore. Write the sentence in which the writer makes this point.

_____

_____

_____

11. Look at the last paragraph. Find the sentence that restates the thesis. Write that sentence here.

_____

_____

_____

Building Better Sentences: For further practice, go to Practice 1 on page 191 in Appendix 1.

The Hook

The opening sentence of any essay is called the **hook**. A hook in writing is used to engage the readers in the subject and keep their attention throughout the essay. Think about the hook while you read the next essay. You will learn more about the hook later in this unit.

ACTIVITY 2 **Studying a Narrative Essay**

This is a descriptive narrative essay about getting results from a university entrance exam. Discuss the Preview Questions with a classmate. Then read the example essay and answer the questions that follow.

Preview Questions

1. Have you ever taken a "high-stakes" exam such as the TOEFL? How did you feel while you waited for the results?

2. What effect can an excellent exam result have on a young person?

Essay 2

July 13, 2013

1   The house was quiet. Of course it was, for everyone was napping on that **steamy** summer day. Normally I would hear my little brothers screaming and playing and my older sisters chatting on their cell phones, but on that day, everything was still. I recall that the temperature that day was 52 degrees Celsius outside, which was hot even for us who live in the desert. The only sound I heard was the air conditioning **struggling** to keep the rooms cool. I was bored and tried to think of something to do. Then the doorbell rang, and my life changed forever.

steamy: very hot and humid

to struggle: to try to do something difficult

2   Because I was the only one awake, I went to the door and answered the bell. There he was—a delivery man holding out an envelope sealed in plastic. "Sign please," he requested. The afternoon sun hurt my eyes, and I **squinted** to find the X that required my signature. I thanked the man and stepped back into the cool **confines** of my living room. Slowly I walked to the sofa and **plopped** down. The letter was addressed to me. I was a fresh high school graduate, and this was the first time that an official letter had my name on it and not my father's.

3   I turned the packet over in my hands a few times, then gently began opening it, careful not to tear anything that might be important. Inside was a letter, a letter containing my future. The university entrance exam results had arrived! As soon as I saw who the letter was from, I started sweating. I got a bit **dizzy**, and my eyes could not focus. Thank goodness that I was sitting down. Then the doubts started. Did I do as well on the exam as I thought I had? What if my scores were too low to enter the university? Would I need to completely change my career plans?

4   So many questions were racing around in my head that I did not hear my mother come down the stairs. "What's that?" she asked. I turned and saw her lovely smile. She had always supported me in my

to squint: strain or narrow your eyes to see something

confines: limits of a place

to plop: drop down

dizzy: wobbly, lightheaded

dreams, especially my dream of studying engineering and becoming one of the few female engineers in my small community. My mouth was so dry that I could barely answer her. I explained about the exam results and how I was afraid to open the letter. She looked at me with that special "mother look" and gave me a small **nod**, basically telling me that everything was going to be all right. With her push, I opened the letter and explored the contents.

to nod: move face up and down to indicate agreement

5   I read the first line over and over again. "We invite you to join our university's engineering program with a full scholarship." I had done it! Not only was I accepted to the university, but my exam scores were so high that I was going to receive a full scholarship. With the letter still in my hand, I jumped off the sofa and ran to show my mother. She screamed with **delight** and hugged me tightly.

delight: happiness, pleasure

6   The noise we made was enough to wake up everyone in the house. Within minutes my father, brothers, and sisters surrounded me in the living room and congratulated me on my accomplishment. That day, July 13, 2013, was the day that changed my life. It was the day that proved to me that if I worked hard enough at something, I would get rewarded.

Post-Reading

1. What is the hook for this essay?

    _____

    _____

    _____

    _____

2. How does this hook try to involve the reader? Do you think that this hook is successful? Why or why not?

    _____

    _____

    _____

3. This essay tells a story. It is an organized sequence of events. This kind of essay is called a narrative essay. Read the list of the main events in the essay below and number the items from 1 to 10 to indicate the order in which the events took place.

    _____ The mother gave the writer courage.

    _____ The writer wondered about her exam score.

    _____ The writer was congratulated by her family.

_____ The writer read the letter.

_____ The writer sat down on the sofa.

_____ The writer's family was napping.

_____ The writer hugged her mother.

_____ The writer was bored.

_____ The writer opened the letter.

_____ The writer answered the door.

4. How many paragraphs are in this essay? _____ In which paragraph does the writer reveal what she wants to study? _____

5. What is the purpose of Paragraph 3?

_____

_____

Building Better Sentences: For further practice, go to Practice 2 on page 192 in Appendix 1.

ACTIVITY 3 Studying a Comparison Essay

Discuss the Preview Questions with a classmate. Then read this comparison essay about two types of lifestyles and answer the questions that follow.

Preview Questions

1. Describe the place where you grew up. Was it the city or the countryside?

2. What were the best and worst things about living there?

Essay 3

The Urban and <u>Rural</u> Divide

1   Imagine life in Tokyo. Now imagine life in a rural Japanese town. Finally, picture life in Cairo, Egypt. Which of these last two places is more different from Tokyo? Many people might mistakenly choose Cairo because it is not found in Japan. However, city **dwellers** all over the world tend to have similar lifestyles, so the biggest differences are found between Tokyo and its smaller neighbor. Urban people and rural people, **regardless of** their country, live quite differently. Perhaps some of the most **notable** differences in the lives of these two groups include the **degree** of friendliness between residents, the **pace** of life, and the variety of available activities.

2   One major difference between growing up in the city and in the country is the degree of friendliness. In large cities, residents often live in huge apartment buildings with hundreds of strangers. These urban apartment dwellers tend to be **wary** of unknown faces and rarely get to

rural: related to the country

a dweller: a person who lives in a place, resident

regardless of: in spite of

notable: important, worthy of notice

the degree: the amount

the pace: the speed, rate

wary: cautious, suspicious

know their neighbors well. The situation in a small town is often just the opposite. Small-town people generally grow up together, attend the same schools, and share the same friends. As a result, rural people are much more likely to treat their neighbors like family and invite them into their homes.

3   Another difference is the pace of life. In the city, life moves very quickly. The streets reflect this hectic pace and are rarely empty, even late at night. City dwellers appear to be racing to get somewhere important. Life for them tends to be a series of **deadlines**. In the country, life is much slower. Even during **peak** hours, traffic jams occur less often than in a city. Stores close in the early evening, and the streets do not come alive until the next morning. The people in small towns or villages seem more relaxed and move in a more leisurely way. The pace of life in these two areas could not be more different.

the deadline: the time limit for doing something

the peak: the highest, the top (amount)

4   A third difference lies in the way people are able to spend their free time. Although life in the city has its **drawbacks**, city dwellers have a much wider choice of activities that they can participate in. For example, they can go to museums, eat in exotic restaurants, attend concerts, and shop in hundreds of stores. The activities available to people in rural areas, however, are much more limited. It is rare to find museums or exotic restaurants there. Concert tours almost never include stops in country towns. Finally, people who enjoy shopping might be disappointed in the small number of stores.

a drawback: a disadvantage, a negative point

5   Life in urban areas and life in rural areas vary in terms of human interaction, pace of life, and daily activities. Other important differences exist, too, but none of these makes one place better than the other. The places are simply different. Only people who have experienced living in both the city and the country can truly appreciate the unique characteristics of each.

Post-Reading

1. What is the topic of this essay?

   _____

2. What is the thesis statement?

   _____

   _____

3. In each paragraph, which type of location is always discussed first—rural or urban? _____

4. Which paragraph talks about activities in each area? _____ Which place offers more

   options for activities? _____

5. In Paragraph 3, the writer contrasts the pace of life in the two areas. Write the supporting sentences
   for the pace of life in each area.

   A. Urban

      1. _____

      2. _____

      3. _____

      4. _____

   B. Rural

      1. _____

      2. _____

      3. _____

      4. _____

   Building Better Sentences: For further practice, go to Practice 3 on page 192 in Appendix 1.

ACTIVITY 4   Studying a Cause-Effect Essay

Discuss the Preview Questions with a classmate. Then read the cause-effect essay and answer the
questions that follow.

Preview Questions

1. Do you think people are healthier now than in the past? Why or why not?

2. What three changes could you make in your lifestyle to become healthier? Be specific.

Cancer Risks

1   Lung cancer kills more people in one year than all criminal and accidental deaths combined. This statistic is shocking, but the good news is that people are now well-informed about the risks connected to lung cancer. They know that their risk of contracting this terrible disease decreases if they either stop smoking or do not smoke at all. Unfortunately, the same cannot be said about other types of cancer. Many people are not aware that their everyday behavior can lead to the development of different forms of cancer. By eating better, exercising regularly, and staying out of the sun, people can reduce their risks of cancer.

2   Instead of foods that are good for them, people often eat unhealthy foods, such as hamburgers, french fries, and pizza. These popular foods contain large amounts of saturated fat, which is one of the worst kinds of fat. Although light and fat-free products are constantly being introduced to the consumer market, many people still buy foods that contain fat because they often taste better. However, eating fatty foods can increase a person's chances for some kinds of cancer. People do not eat as many fresh vegetables and fresh fruits as they used to. Instead, they now eat a lot more processed foods that do not contain natural **fiber**. Lack of fiber in a person's diet can increase the chance of **colon** cancer. In the past, people with less information about nutrition actually had better diets than people do today. They also had fewer cases of cancer.

3   Many people today are overweight, and being overweight has been connected to some kinds of cancer. Since television sets are now a standard piece of furniture in most living rooms, people spend more time sitting down and mindlessly eating snacks than they did in the past. The first generation of TV watchers started the **couch potato boom**, and today's couch potatoes are bigger than ever. Health experts warn that being overweight is a risk not only for heart disease but also for certain kinds of cancer. The best way to **attain** a healthy weight is for people to **cut back on** the amount of food that they consume and to exercise regularly. It is not possible to do only one of these and lose weight permanently. The improved diet must be **in conjunction with** regular exercise. In the past, people did more physical activity than people do today. For example, people used to walk to work; now almost no one does. In addition, people had jobs that required more physical labor. Now many people have desk jobs that require sitting in front of computers.

4   Finally, health officials are gravely concerned by the **astounding** rise in the cases of skin cancer. Many societies value a tanned complexion, so on weekends people tend to **flock to** the beach or swimming pools and lie in the sun. Many of these people do not use a

fiber: a plant material that is good for the digestive system

the colon: an organ in the digestive system

a couch potato: a person who spends a lot of time on the couch watching TV

a boom: a sudden increase in popularity

to attain: to achieve

to cut back on: to reduce the amount (of something)

in conjunction with: at the same time as, together with

astounding: amazing, surprising

to flock to: to go to a place in large numbers (as birds do)

safe sunscreen, and the result is that they often get sunburned. Sunburn damages the skin, and repeated damage may lead to skin cancer later in life. Once the damage is done, it cannot be undone. Thus, prevention is important. In the past, people did not lie in direct sunlight for long periods of time, and skin cancer was not as **prevalent** as it is now. People have started to listen to doctors' warnings about this situation, and more and more people are using proper sunscreens. Unfortunately, millions of people already have this potential cancer problem in their skin and may develop cancer later.

prevalent: common

5   Cancer has been around since the earliest days of human existence, but only recently has the public been made aware of some of the risk factors involved. Antismoking campaigns can be seen everywhere—on billboards, in television commercials, on the radio, and in newsprint. If the same amount of attention were given to proper diets, exercise, and sunscreens, perhaps the number of overall cancer cases could be reduced.

Post-Reading

1. What is the writer's main message in this essay? _Everyday behavior can lead to the development of different forms of cancer._

2. What is the thesis statement of this essay?

   By eating better, exercising regularly and staying out of the sun, people can reduce their risks of cancer.

3. The thesis statement should tell the reader how the essay will be organized. What do you know about the organization of the essay from the thesis statement?

   Eating better, exercising regularly and staying out of sun.

4. In Paragraph 2, the writer states that many people eat unhealthy food. What supporting information explains why this food is not healthy?

   Hamburgers, french fries and pizza. These popular foods contain large amounts of saturated fat.

5. In Paragraph 2, the writer also explains why people enjoy eating unhealthy foods. Write the reason here.

   They often taste better.

Building Better Sentences: For further practice, go to Practice 4 on page 193 in Appendix 1.

ACTIVITY 5 **Studying a Comparison/Argument Essay**

Discuss the Preview Questions with a classmate. Then read the essay on educational choices and answer the questions that follow.

Preview Questions

1. What do you know about community colleges? How are they different from universities?

2. What are some things that students consider when they are choosing a college?

An Alternative to University Education

1   A high school diploma is not the end of many people's education these days. High school students who want to continue their education generally choose one of two routes after graduation. Some students **opt to** attend a community college and then transfer to a university, while others go directly to a university. Making this difficult choice requires a great deal of careful thought. However, if the choice is based on three specific factors, **namely**, cost, location, and quality of education, students will quickly see the advantages that attending a community college offers.

2   Attending a community college is much cheaper than attending a university. For example, **tuition** at a local community college might cost $3,000 per year, especially for residents of the area. The same classes taken at a nearby university could cost over $25,000. In addition, a university would charge more for parking, photocopying at the library, cafeteria food, and campus health clinic services. No matter how the total bill is calculated or what is included, it is more expensive to study at a university.

to opt to: to choose to (do something)

namely: such as, for example, that is

the tuition: money paid for classes

3   Studying at a community college can be more convenient because of its location. Going to a university often requires recent high school graduates to live far from home, and many of them are **reluctant** to do so. These students are only seventeen or eighteen years old and may have very little experience with being away from home. It is often difficult for these young people to suddenly find themselves far away from their families. In addition, very few parents are prepared to send their teenagers to distant universities. Because almost every area has a community college, students who opt to go to a community college first can continue to be near their families for two more years.

reluctant: hesitant

4   Finally, there are educational benefits to attending a community college. University life is very different from community college life. A university campus offers a large variety of sports events and social activities, and students can easily become distracted from their studies. Community colleges, which typically have fewer students and extracurricular activities, may be a better environment for serious study. In addition, the library facilities at a community college, though not as large as those at a university, are more than sufficient for the kind of work that is required in first- or second-year courses. Class size is also an issue to consider. Introductory courses at universities often have 50, 60, or even 100 students. In such large classes, student-teacher interaction is **minimal**, and learning can be more difficult for some students. Finally, the teaching at community colleges is often better than the teaching at a university. Professors at community colleges often have the same **credentials** as those at universities, but community college professors spend most of their time teaching instead of conducting research, as university professors have to do.

minimal: the least amount possible

a credential: a qualification

5   The decision to enter a university directly or to attend a community college for the first two years after high school can be difficult. Community colleges are not as glamorous as large universities. They are often **perceived** as second-rate alternatives to the more well-known universities. However, based on the three important factors outlined above—cost, location, and quality of education—it is clear that for many students, choosing a community college is the smarter thing to do.

to perceive: to see, to believe to be

Post-Reading

1. What two things are being compared in this essay?

Community College and University.

Which one does the writer think is better?

Community College

2. What is the organization of this essay? Fill in the blanks of this simple outline with the words that are missing.

Topic: The Advantages of Community Colleges

  I. Introduction (Paragraph 1)

   Thesis statement: _However, if the choice is based on three specific factors, namely, cost, location and quality of education_

 II. Body

   A. Paragraph 2 topic: _Cost_

     1. Tuition

       a. Community college: $ _3,000_

       b. _University_ : $ _25,000_

     2. Other costs

       a. Parking

       b. _Photocopying at the library._

       c. Health clinic services

       d. _Cafeteria food._

   B. Paragraph 3 topic: Location

     1. Better for students

       a. _college._

       b. _University._

     2. Better for parents

   C. Paragraph 4 topic: _Education benefits. differences_

     1. Distractions of university

     2. Community college: Quiet campus

     3. _fewer students_

     4. Class size

     5. Quality of teaching

III. Conclusion (Paragraph 5)

3. The writer discusses three factors—cost, location, and quality of education—in the decision about what kind of college to attend. Can you think of two other factors that the writer could have used?

_____

_____

4. Before you read this essay, did you know much about this topic? What was your opinion before you read this essay? (Check all possible answers.)

___✓___ I thought that attending a university directly after high school was better.

_____ I thought that attending a community college after high school was better.

___✓___ I thought that a university offered a better education than a community college.

_____ I thought that a community college offered a better education than a university.

_____ I thought that a university was cheaper than a community college.

___✓___ I thought that a community college was cheaper than a university.

_____ I did not know much about university education.

___✓___ I did not know much about community college education.

5. Did your opinion about community colleges change after you read "An Alternative to University Education"? In other words, did the writer persuade you to change your mind about community colleges?

Yes my opinion change.

6. Which part of the essay was the most persuasive for you?

The cost.

7. If your answer to question 5 is *yes*, tell why your opinion changed. If your answer to question 5 is *no*, write three specific reasons why you still believe a university is a better choice.

Because I studied in University so, I did have any Idea about the collge.

_____

_____

Building Better Sentences: For further practice, go to Practice 5 on page 194 in Appendix 1.

Writing the Introduction

The **introduction** is the first part of an essay, usually the first paragraph. The introduction does not have to be written first, however. Some writers design and write this part of the essay last or at another point in their writing process.

From the basic outline that follows, you can see how the introduction fits into the essay.

    I. Introduction (usually one paragraph)

   II. Body (one to four paragraphs)

  III. Conclusion (usually one paragraph)

There are many ways to write an introduction. Some writers begin with a question. Other writers give background information about the topic. The kind of introduction you choose depends on how you want to present the topic and the kind of essay you decide to write.

What Is in the Introduction?

The introduction for most essays is one paragraph. This introductory paragraph usually consists of three parts:

$$
\text{INTRODUCTION} = \begin{cases} 1. & \text{The hook} \\ 2. & \text{Connecting information} \\ 3. & \text{The thesis statement} \end{cases}
$$

Now look at each of these parts to see what they are and how they work in the introduction.

The Hook

The **hook** is the opening statement or statements of an essay. Just as people use a hook at the end of a fishing pole to catch a fish, writers use a hook to catch the readers' attention. If a hook does its job well, readers will stay with the essay and want to read the rest of it. The hook is the one part of any essay where you can be as creative as you want.

There are many different ways to write a hook.

1. **Ask a question.** If readers want to know the answer to the question, they are "hooked" and will read the essay. For example, a writer might begin an essay about the need for more regulations on technology usage with this question:

   How many people begin their mornings—every day—by checking their cell phones?

Most readers will not know the answer to this question, but they will probably be interested and want to find out more about the topic.

2. **Use an interesting observation.** Here is an example:

   European economists are not sleeping well these days.

This observation makes readers want to know why economists are not sleeping well. This hook leads to the main idea of the essay, which will highlight the three main causes of recession in Europe.

Here is *another example* of an observation hook full of interesting details that leads readers to the topic of international trade:

> The average Canadian is proud to be Canadian and can easily talk about the benefits of living in Canada. However, many Canadians drive Japanese or German cars to work every morning. They wear cotton shirts made in Honduras and pants made in Bangladesh. Their dinner salad may contain tomatoes from California and salad dressing from France. Before going to bed, Canadians will most likely watch their favorite TV programs on a Japanese or Korean television.

3. **Use a unique scenario to catch readers' attention.** Here is an example:

> Traveling at more than one hundred miles an hour, he feels as though he is not moving. He is engulfed in complete silence. For a moment, it is as if he has entered another dimension.

Are you hooked? Do you want to read the rest of the essay? This essay is about the exciting sport of skydiving.

4. **Begin with a famous quote.** Study this example:

> "I have a dream."

Many readers may think that this hook will lead into a discussion of Martin Luther King, Jr.'s life or his struggles. In fact, this hook begins an essay on the topic of sleep patterns.

5. **Use a surprising or shocking statistic.** Here are two examples:

> The divorce rate in the United States is well over 50 percent.

> If world temperatures continue to rise, Singapore and New York may be under water by the year 2050.

Writer's Note

Hook versus Main Idea

In English writing, the main idea, or thesis, of an essay is usually in the introduction, but it is generally not the first sentence. (The hook is usually the first sentence or the first few sentences.) You could begin an essay with a sentence stating the main idea:

> This essay will talk about common methods of curbing one's appetite.

> or

> There are three ways to curb your appetite.

However, in academic writing, beginning with a sentence that plainly states the main idea is not preferred because it gives away the main idea of the essay too soon. As a result, your readers may not be interested in reading the rest of the essay. Stating the main idea will not grab your readers' attention, so be sure to begin your essay with an interesting hook.

Connecting Information

After the hook, the writer usually writes **connecting information**, which is three to five sentences that help connect the reader to the topic. These sentences can be background information about the topic or they can be examples. The following sentences from Essay 1 on page 6 give examples of how Cinderella probably spent her days before she met the prince:

> Her daily routine was not glamorous. She did everything from sweeping the floors to cooking the meals. If someone had asked Cinderella which chores she did not particularly like, she probably would have answered, "Why, none, of course. Housework is my duty!"

From these sentences, the reader has a good idea of what the topic might be—unpleasant household chores.

The Thesis Statement

The **thesis statement** is usually the last part of the introduction. It is usually one sentence. In the thesis statement, the writer tells the reader what to expect in the essay. Basically, there are two kinds of thesis statements—**direct** and **indirect**. (They may also be called stated and implied thesis statements.)

1. **Direct Thesis Statement.** Some writers want to give a specific outline of their essays in their thesis statements. Read the following example:

> The main problems facing this nation are a lack of job opportunities for citizens, government corruption, and limited university programs for poor students.

From this statement, the reader knows that the body of the essay has three main parts. The first part will discuss job opportunities, the second part will talk about government corruption, and the last part will talk about university programs for poor students. This kind of thesis statement is called a stated thesis.

2. **Indirect Thesis Statement.** Other writers are not so direct. Discussing a similar topic as the previous example, these writers might use this statement:

> There are three important problems facing the nation today that require immediate attention.

From this statement, the reader expects to find a discussion of problems in his or her country. The reader is not given the specific information that will follow in the essay, but the general topic is clear. In this case, the reader must continue reading to find the supporting ideas of the argument. This kind of thesis statement is called an indirect thesis.

ACTIVITY 6 · Practice with Hooks

In this argument essay, the writer argues that mandatory retirement should be abolished. The essay begins with the connecting information. First, read the entire essay. Then go back and write two possible hooks that would capture the readers' attention. When you are done, share the three hooks that you wrote with your classmates. Are any of them similar? Explain why you think your hooks will grab readers' attention.

No More Mandatory Retirement

1   Hook 1: <u>Are you ready for retirement?</u>

_____

_____

_____

_____

_____

_____

Hook 2: _____

_____

_____

_____

_____

_____

Traditionally, people retire from their jobs when they reach the age of 65. In some jobs, this is not an option but a requirement. **Mandatory** retirement for capable workers is wrong because it violates personal choice, discriminates against senior citizens, and wastes valuable skills as well as money.

mandatory: necessary

2   One reason that mandatory retirement is wrong is that it takes away an individual's personal choice of either continuing to work or retiring. The older working person should have the right to choose his or her retirement age. A person's right to life, liberty, and the pursuit of happiness (as written in the Declaration of Independence) is a very special thing. Forced retirement takes away people's **livelihood**, deprives them of their freedom to choose how to spend their time, and prevents them from pursuing happiness.

a livelihood: source of income

3   Second, mandatory retirement is surely a form of age discrimination. A young person might wonder why an older worker should be kept on the payroll when the company could hire someone who is younger and more creative. However, a younger person would not necessarily be a better or more creative worker. Age does not indicate the quality of a person's work. Many well-known artists, politicians, and writers developed their best works after the age of 60. The common belief that a person's mind slows down after a certain age is nothing but a **misconception**.

a misconception: error, false impression

4   In addition to the previous two points, quality of work is another important issue. Older employees have knowledge and experience that can truly be beneficial to a company. Unfortunately, many employers **disregard** this fact. Captain Al Haynes, aged 58, was able to land a DC-10 that was out of control so that 186 of the 296 people aboard survived when it crashed. The aircraft manufacturer simulated the same situation 45 times, and not one time did they have a successful landing. Safety experts agree that the high survival rate among the passengers on the flight was due to Captain Haynes's aviation skills. It is doubtful that a less experienced pilot could have accomplished this feat. However, two years later, Captain Haynes had to retire because he had reached the age of 60, the mandatory retirement age for pilots in the United States.

to disregard: ignore, pay no attention to

5   Many people, especially fresh college graduates, do not agree that retirement should be an option. They are worried that if older workers are allowed to continue in their jobs, there will not be enough openings for younger people. However, is there really a danger that older people will take away job opportunities from younger people? This situation is unlikely because younger workers and older workers rarely compete for the same jobs. The reality is that older workers rarely seek entry-level positions. Therefore, employers should start looking for ways to attract experienced workers, not retire them.

6   In conclusion, the age of retirement should be **determined** by an individual's economic need, health status, and personal preference. People's lives are their own, and they should be allowed to live them to their fullest potential. Without a doubt, mandatory retirement goes against **fulfilling** this potential and should not be a part of modern society.

determined: decided, concluded

fulfilling: satisfying, pleasing

Answer these questions about the thesis statement in "No More Mandatory Retirement."

1. What is the thesis statement in the essay? _Mandatory retirement for capable workers is wrong because it violates personal choice, discriminates against senior citizens, and wastes valuable skills as well as money._

2. Is this a direct or indirect thesis statement? _Indirect thesis statement._

    _____

3. Rewrite the thesis statement using the alternative form. _____

    There are many reson for retirement workers is wrong.

    _____

    _____

Building Better Sentences: For further practice, go to Practice 6 on page 195 in Appendix 1.

ACTIVITY 8 More Practice with Hooks

This comparison essay compares two different types of jobs. The essay begins with the connecting information. First, read the whole essay. Then go back and write two possible hooks that would capture the readers' attention.

Essay 7

The Truth about Coaches and Business Managers

1 Hook 1: _Do you know there are many r. similarities between the job of an athletic coach and business manger?_

    _____

    _____

    _____

    Hook 2: _____

    _____

    _____

    _____

    _____

    _____

Coaches work outdoors while business managers stay in offices. Coaches train athletes' bodies, but managers are more focused on detail-oriented matters. These differences, however, **pale in comparison** to the similarities shared by the two professions, for the main functions of athletic team coaches and business managers are very closely related.

2   One of the most **fundamental** similarities between athletic team coaches and business managers is the task of leading the team members or employees. Coaches are responsible for training their athletes and focusing on each individual's strengths and weaknesses. Coaches also give directions to their players to improve their performance and commonly give feedback after a game. Similarly, business managers are responsible for the proper training of their employees. Managers use their people skills to **ensure** that each worker is put in the job that suits his or her abilities best. In addition, managers typically give periodic reviews of their employees as feedback on their job performance.

3   Another important similarity between the two professions is the ability to solve problems between teammates or employees. Athletes tend to be very competitive, and often this competitiveness leads to arguments in practice and during games. Coaches know that this behavior is not productive in leading the team to victory, so they often act as **intermediaries**. They listen to both sides and usually come up with words of wisdom or advice to straighten out the problem. In the same way, a manager is often asked to mediate between two or more employees who might not be getting along in the office. Managers know that teamwork is vital to productivity, so they are trained to make sure that the workplace runs smoothly.

to pale in comparison: to be weak compared to something else

a fundamental: basic

to ensure: guarantee; make sure

an intermediary: mediators; people who try to get two groups together

4   Finally, both coaches and managers must represent their subordinates to the members of higher management. Many social groups function as **hierarchies**, and the locker room and office are no different. Coaches are regularly asked to report to the team owners with updates on the season. They write up reports to keep the owners informed about who is doing well, who is injured, and who is not performing **up to par**. In addition, they serve as the players' spokespersons. If players have a **particular** problem related to something other than their athletic performance, it is usually the coaches who end up speaking with the owners on the players' behalf. Like coaches, business managers are the links between the CEOs and lower-level employees. The business managers are given the tasks of overseeing employees and serving as go-betweens. Top management wants to remain aware of what is happening in the company, but they usually do not have the time to deal with such details. Business managers, therefore, serve as spokespeople to both ends of the hierarchy.

a hierarchy: chains of command

up to par: performing adequately

particular: specific

5   On the surface, the two occupations seem completely unrelated. The coach works outdoors and handles the pressures of physical exercise and game strategies while the business manager works in a formal environment surrounded by modern technology. Upon further **inspection**, however, these two occupations are very closely related. Both coaches and managers are the glue that holds the members of the team together.

an inspection: examination; check

In pairs or small groups, share the three hooks that you wrote with your classmates. Are any of them similar? Explain why you think your hooks will attract readers' attention.

ACTIVITY 9 **Thesis Statement Questions**

Answer these questions about the thesis statement in "The Truth about Coaches and Business Managers."

1. What is the thesis statement in the essay?

These difference however pale in comparison to the similarities shared by tow professions, for the mine functons of athletic team chaches and business managers are vary closely related.

2. Is this a direct or indirect thesis? _____ Give the reason for your answer.

Indirect use, telling about different and similarties.

3. Rewrite the thesis statement using the alternative form.

There are many similarities between coaches and business managers.

Building Better Sentences: For further practice, go to Practice 7 on page 196 in Appendix 1.

Writing the Body

The body of an essay is its main part. It usually consists of three or four paragraphs between the introduction and the conclusion. The body follows a plan of organization that the writer usually determines before he or she starts writing. This organization varies depending on the kind of essay the writer is writing.

Writers can write the organizational plan of an essay in an **outline**. There are different levels of outlining. A **general outline** includes the main points, while a **specific**, or **detailed**, **outline** includes notes on even the smallest pieces of information that will go into the essay. It is much easier to write an essay from a specific outline than from a general outline. However, most writers start with a general outline first and then add details.

Writer's Note

Using an Outline

The best essays have well-planned outlines that are prepared before the writer starts writing. By spending more time in this pre-writing stage, the writer can organize his or her thoughts, often moving them around until the information looks cohesive in the outline. Once it is time to write the essay, the organization and flow of ideas will have already been reviewed.

Here is a general outline and a specific outline for Essay 7, "The Truth about Coaches and Business Managers," on pages 27–29. Read and compare the two outlines.

General Outline	Specific Outline
I. Introduction	**I.** Introduction
A. Hook: Pose a question	**A.** Hook: Are athletic coaches similar to business managers?
B. Connecting information	**B.** Connecting information: They work in different places and focus on different jobs.
C. Thesis: Similarities in coaches' and managers' jobs	**C.** Thesis: The two professions share many similarities, because the main functions of athletic team coaches and business managers are very closely related.

General Outline	Specific Outline
II. Body	**II.** Body

A. Similarity 1: Leading the athletes and employees	**A.** Similarity 1: Leading the athletes and employees
	      1. Coaches train athletes
	         a. Focus on strengths
	         b. Focus on weaknesses
	         c. Give feedback
	      2. Managers train employees
	         a. Put employees in jobs that fit them best
	         b. Perform job reviews

B. Similarity 2: Solving problems	**B.** Similarity 2: Solving problems
	      1. Coaches listen to athletes
	         a. Stop fights
	         b. Act as go-betweens
	      2. Managers mediate in office
	         a. Stress importance of teamwork with employees
	         b. Try to get officemates to cooperate

C. Similarity 3: Representing the athletes and employees	**C.** Similarity 3: Representing the athletes and employees
	      1. Coaches to owners
	         a. Give updates to owners
	         b. Discuss athletes' problems
	      2. Managers to CEOs
	         a. Maintain control on behalf of the bosses
	         b. Update the CEOs on employee issues

III. Conclusion: Focus on maintaining communication	**III.** Conclusion: Both careers are fundamental in improving communication and keeping the team together

ACTIVITY 10 **Making a General Outline**

Here is a general outline for Narrative Essay 2, "July 13, 2013," on pages 9–11. Read the essay again and complete this outline.

Title: _____

  I. Introduction (Paragraph 1)

     A. Hook: Give background information

     B. Connecting information

     C. Thesis statement: _____

_____

  II. Body

     A. Paragraph 2 topic sentence: Because I was the only one awake, I went to the door and answered the bell.

B. Paragraph 3 topic sentence: _____

_____

C. Paragraph 4 topic sentence: _____

_____

D. Paragraph 5 topic sentence: I read the first line over and over again.

III. Conclusion (Paragraph 6)

  A. End of action

  B. Restatement of thesis

  C. Specific Outline

ACTIVITY 11 **Making a Specific Outline**

Here is a specific outline for Classification Essay 1, "Cinderella and Her Tedious Household Chores," on pages 6–7. Read the essay again and complete this outline. You may use complete sentences if you wish, but be sure to include all of the specific information.

Title: _Cinderelland Household chores_____

  I. Introduction (Paragraph 1)

    A. Hook: _____

_____

    B. Connecting information: _____

_____

_____

    C. Thesis statement: _____

_____

  II. Body

    A. Paragraph 2

      1. Topic sentence (Chore #1): _one of the most_____

_____

SUPPORT

      2. Supporting ideas

        a. Attention to detail

        (1) Smoothing out the fabric

        (2) Following the seams

        (3) _____

        (4) _____

    b. Problem: _____

    _____

B. Paragraph 3

    1. Topic sentence (Chore #2): _____

    2. Supporting ideas

        a. Why we cannot depend on dishwashers

        b. Negative aspects of this chore

        (1) Elbow grease

        (2) _____

        (3) _____

C. Paragraph 4

    1. Topic sentence (Chore #3): _____

    2. Supporting ideas _____

        a. Tasks

        (1) _____

        (2) Cleaning the sink

        (3) Cleaning the toilet

        b. Negative aspects

        (1) Bathroom is full of germs

        (2) _____

        c. Positive aspect: _____

III. Conclusion (Paragraph 5)

    A. Maintaining a house includes chores.

    B. People get through the three tedious chores by taking pride in doing a good job.

Writing the Conclusion

Some people think that writing the conclusion is the hardest part of writing an essay. For others, writing the conclusion is easy. When you write a conclusion, follow these guidelines:

1. Let the reader know that this is the conclusion. You can mark the conclusion with some kind of transition or connector that tells the reader that this is the final paragraph of the essay.

> For a more complete list of connectors, see the *Brief Writer's Handbook with Activities*, pages 180–181.

Here are some examples:

In conclusion,   From the information given,   To summarize,

Sometimes the first sentence of the conclusion restates the thesis or main idea of the essay:

As previously noted, there are numerous problems that new parents face today.

2. Do not introduce new information in the conclusion. The conclusion should help the reader to reconsider the main ideas that you have given in the essay. Any new information in the concluding paragraph will sound like a continuation of the body of the essay.

3. Many writers find the conclusion difficult to write. It requires a great deal of thought and creativity, just as writing a good hook or thesis statement does. The kind of essay you are writing may determine the way you end the essay; however, the following ideas can be helpful for any essay.

   a. The final sentence or sentences of an essay often give a suggestion, an opinion, or a prediction about the topic of the essay.

   - **Suggestion:** In order for young people to successfully learn a language, parents need to encourage them at an early age.

   - **Opinion:** Learning a second language at an early age is, in effect, a smart choice.

   - **Prediction:** If more young people were bilingual, perhaps they would better understand the complex world around them.

   b. Sometimes the final sentence or sentences simply say that the issue has been discussed in the essay with so many strong, persuasive facts that the answer to the issue is now clear.

   Once aware of this information, any reader would agree that bilingual education is an excellent educational opportunity.

Writer's Note

Checking the First and Last Paragraphs

After you write your essay, read the introductory paragraph and the concluding paragraph. These two paragraphs should contain similar information.

Building Better Vocabulary

ACTIVITY 12 **Word Associations**

Circle the word or phrase that is most closely related to the word or phrase on the left. If necessary, use a dictionary to check the meaning of words you do not know.

	A	**B**
1. a chore	pleasant	(unpleasant)
2. struggle	difficult	(easy)
3. nod	no	yes
4. rural	few people	many people
5. wary	confident	suspicious
6. tuition	money	work
7. reluctant*	hesitant	(repetitive)
8. a drawback	negative	(positive)
9. a routine	habit	(surprising)
10. prevalent	(common)	rare

*Indicates words that are part of the Academic Word List. See pages 183–184 for a complete list.

ACTIVITY 13 **Using Collocations**

Fill in each blank with the word on the left that most naturally completes the phrase on the right. If necessary, use a dictionary to check the meaning of words you do not know.

1. computer / daily	on a ___daily___ basis
2. has / makes	it ___makes___ sense
3. by / with	in conjunction ___by___
4. claim / entail	some people ___claim___ that
5. as / with	the same credentials ___with___
6. detergent / grease	elbow ___grease___

7. against / of   to discriminate _against_

8. fundamental / higher   _higher_ management

9. thick / wide   a _wide_ variety of

10. tackle / wrinkle   to _tackle_ a difficult task

Original Student Writing

Understanding the Writing Process: The Seven Steps

There are many ways to write, but most good writers follow certain steps in the writing process.

Step 1: Choose a topic. Ideally the topic should be something that interests you.

Step 2: Brainstorm. Write down as many ideas as you can about your chosen topic; you will move things around and change ideas as you reach Step 3.

Step 3: Outline. Once you have a topic and a thesis statement, it is time to put your ideas into a logical format. Write an outline to help you organize how you will present your ideas.

Step 4: Write the first draft. Use the information from your brainstorming session and your outline to write a first draft. At this stage, do not worry about errors in your writing. Focus on putting your ideas into sentences.

Step 5: Get feedback from a peer. The more feedback you have, the better. Your classmates can help you with the content and organization of your paper, as can your instructor.

Step 6: Revise the first draft. Based on the feedback you receive, consider making some changes.

Step 7: Proofread the final draft. Review the final paper before you turn it in. Be sure it is typed, double-spaced, and free of any grammatical and spelling errors.

For more detailed information on the seven steps of the writing process, see the *Brief Writer's Handbook with Activities*, beginning on page 156.

ACTIVITY 14   **Essay Writing Practice**

Write an essay on one of the following suggested topics. Depending on the topic that you choose, you may need to do some research. Use at least two of the vocabulary words or phrases presented in Activities 12 and 13. Underline these words and phrases in your essay. Before you write, be sure to refer to the seven steps in the writing process.

If you need ideas for words and phrases, see the Useful Vocabulary for Better Writing on pages 185–188.

الأفكار العامة

Additional Topics for Writing

PHOTO
TOPIC: Look at the photograph on pages 2–3. Describe a festival or celebration in your culture. Discuss how it is celebrated and what it means to people.

TOPIC 2: Write an essay about an important event that changed your life, such as marriage, the birth of a child, moving to a foreign country, or the loss of someone close to you.

TOPIC 3: Many recent developments in technology, such as the smartphone or tablet computer, have changed our lives. Write an essay in which you discuss the effects of one recent technological invention on society.

TOPIC 4: Some people say that individuals are born with their intelligence and that outside factors do not affect intelligence very much. They believe that nature (what we are born with) is more important than nurture (environment). Other people say that intelligence is mainly the result of the interaction between people and their environment. These people believe that nurture is more important than nature. Write an essay in which you defend one of these points of view.

TOPIC 5: Write about a movie that you saw recently. Begin by summarizing the story; then tell what you liked and did not like about it.

Timed Writing

How quickly can you write in English? There are many times when you must write quickly, such as on a test. It is important to feel comfortable during those times. Timed-writing practice can make you feel better about writing quickly in English.

1. Take out a piece of paper.

2. Read the essay guidelines and the writing prompt.

3. Write a basic outline, including the thesis and your three main points.

4. Write a five-paragraph essay.

5. You have 40 minutes to write your essay.

Essay Guidelines

- Remember to give your essay a title.

- Double-space your essay.

- Write as legibly as possible (if you are not using a computer).

- Select an appropriate principle of organization for your topic.

- Include a short introduction (with a thesis statement), three body paragraphs, and a conclusion.

- Try to give yourself a few minutes before the end of the activity to review your work. Check for spelling, verb tense, and subject-verb agreement mistakes.

What are the benefits of knowing a second language?

National Geographic explorers Beverly and Dereck Joubert are in Duba Plains, Botswana. Their accomplishments include launching the Big Cats Initiative, a global awareness program to protect lions, tigers, cheetahs, leopards, and jaguars.

OBJECTIVES To learn how to write a narrative essay
To use connectors and time relationship words
To understand adjective clauses

Can you write a story about a person who has done something inspirational?

What Is a Narrative Essay?

A **narrative** essay tells a story. In fact, *narrative* is another word for *story*. In this unit, you will learn how to organize and write a narrative essay. Even though the narrative essay has the same basic form as most other academic essays, it allows the writer to be a little more creative than academic essays usually do. Narratives can tell long stories or just a few minutes' worth of excitement. While the narrative essay has a particular structure, narrative ideas are often used in different writing tasks, such as argument or compare-contrast.

Structure of a Story

Several important elements make up a good story:

Setting   The setting is the location where the action in a story takes place.

Theme   The theme is the basic idea of the story. Very often the theme will deal with a topic that is common in life or human nature, such as independence, envy, courage, failure, and success.

Mood   The mood is the feeling or atmosphere that the writer creates for the story. It could be happy, hopeful, suspenseful, or scary. Both the setting and descriptive vocabulary create the mood in a narrative.

Characters   The characters are the people in the story. They are affected by the mood of the story, and they react to the events in which they are involved.

Plot   The plot is what happens in the story, that is, the sequence of events. The plot often includes a climax or turning point at which the characters or events change.

Just like other types of essays, an effective narrative essay also includes these elements:

- a **thesis** that sets up the action in the introduction

- **transition sentences** that connect events and help the reader follow the story

- a **conclusion** that ends the story action and provides a moral, prediction, or revelation

The Introduction

The **introduction** of a narrative essay is the paragraph that begins your story. In the introduction, you describe the setting, introduce the characters, and prepare your audience for the action to come. Of course, the introduction should have a hook and a thesis.

The Narrative Hook

You learned in Unit 1 that the **hook** in an essay is the part of the introduction—usually the first few sentences—that grabs readers' attention. Hooks are especially important in narrative essays because they help set the stage for the story. The hook makes readers start guessing about what will happen next. Let's look at the hook from Essay 8 that you will read in Activity 2.

> I had never been more anxious in my life. I had just spent the last three endless hours trying to get to the airport so that I could travel home.

Does this hook make you want to know what happened to the narrator? The hook should make the reader ask *wh-* questions about the essay. You may have thought of questions like these when you read the preceding hook:

- <u>Who</u> is the narrator and <u>why</u> is he or she anxious?
- <u>Where</u> is the airport?
- <u>What</u> made the trip to the airport seem endless?
- <u>Why</u> is this person going home?

ACTIVITY 1 Identifying Hooks

Read the sentences below. Which three sentences would <u>not</u> be good hooks for a narrative essay? Put a ✓ next to these sentences. Be ready to explain why you think these sentences do not work well as hooks for narrative essays.

1. _____ The roar of race-car engines ripped through the blazing heat of the day.

2. _____ It was freezing on that sad December day.

3. _____ After my brother's accident, I sat alone in the hospital waiting room.

4. _____ My friend and I should not have been walking home alone so late on that dark winter night.

5. __✓__ Whales are by far the largest marine mammals.

6. __✓__ She gave her friend a birthday gift.

7. _____ The gleaming snow lay over the treacherous mountain like a soft white blanket, making the terrain seem safe instead of deadly.

8. __✓__ The Russian dictionary that we use in our language class has 500 pages.

9. _____ Amber never expected to hear the deadly sound of a rattlesnake in her kitchen garden.

10. _____ A shot rang out in the silence of the night.

The Thesis

In most types of essays, the **thesis** states the main idea of the essay and tells what the organization of the information will be. However, in a narrative essay, the thesis introduces the action that begins in the first paragraph of the essay. Look at these example thesis statements:

> Now, as I watched the bus driver set my luggage on the airport sidewalk, I realized that my frustration had only just begun.

> I wanted my mother to watch me race down the steep hill, so I called out her name and then nudged my bike forward.

> Because his pride would not allow him to apologize, Ken now had to fight the bully, and he was pretty sure that he would not win.

These thesis statements do not tell the reader what happens. They only introduce the action that will follow. The paragraphs in the body will develop the story.

The Body

The **body** of your narrative essay contains most of the plot—the supporting information. The action in the plot can be organized in many different ways. One way is **chronological** or time order. In this method, each paragraph gives more information about the story as it proceeds in time—the first paragraph usually describes the first event, the second paragraph describes the second event, and so on.

Transitional Sentences

In an essay with chronological organization, each paragraph ends with a **transitional sentence**. Transitional sentences have two purposes: (1) to signal the end of the action in one paragraph, and (2) to provide a link to the action of the next paragraph. These sentences are vital because they give your story unity and allow the reader to follow the action easily. The following example is from Essay 8 on page 43, Paragraphs 2 and 3. Notice how the ideas in the last sentence of Paragraph 2 (the transitional sentence, underlined) and the first sentence of Paragraph 3 (underlined) are connected.

---

2   This was my first visit to the international terminal of the airport, and nothing was familiar. I could not make sense of any of the signs. Where was the check-in counter? Where should I take my luggage? I had no idea where the immigration line was. I began to panic. What time was it? Where was my plane? I had to find help because I could not be late!

3   I tried to ask a passing businessman for help, but my words all came out wrong. He just scowled and walked away. What had happened? I had been in this country for a whole semester, and I could not even remember how to ask for directions. This was awful! Another bus arrived at the terminal, and the passengers stepped off carrying all sorts of luggage. Here was my chance! I could follow them to the right place, and I would not have to say a word.

The Conclusion

Like academic essays, narrative essays need to have concluding ideas. In the **conclusion**, you finish describing the action in the essay. The final sentence can have two functions:

1. It can deliver the **moral** of the story by telling the reader what the character(s) learned from the experience.

2. It can make a **prediction** or a **revelation** (disclosure of something that was not known before) about future actions that will happen as a result of the events in the story.

Look at these examples:

Moral   The little boy had finally learned that telling the truth was the most important thing to do.

Prediction   I can only hope that one day I will be able to do the same for another traveler who is suffering through a terrible journey.

Revelation   Every New Year's Eve, my wife and I return to that magical spot and remember the selfless act that saved our lives.

Writer's Note

Storytelling Tip

If you describe the sights, smells, and sounds of the story, you will bring the story alive for the reader. Try to include a few adjectives in your sentences. The more descriptive the information, the more the reader will connect with the story you are telling. Make readers feel that they are there with you as you experience what you are describing.

In the following example, the writer uses adjectives (underlined) to add depth to the story by giving additional information.

> I walked into the noisy classroom and looked for a place to sit down. In the back of the well-lit room, I saw an old wooden desk and walked toward it. After a few moments, the anxious students quieted down when they observed the prim English teacher enter the room.

ACTIVITY 2 Studying a Narrative Essay

Discuss the Preview Questions with a classmate. Then read the essay and answer the questions that follow.

Preview Questions

1. Have you ever had trouble getting from one place to another while traveling? Where were you going? What happened that made this travel difficult?

2. Can everyday people be considered heroes? What do you consider to be a heroic act?

Essay 8

Frustration at the Airport

1   I had never been more anxious in my life. I had just spent the last three endless hours trying to get to the airport so that I could travel home. Now, as I watched the bus driver set my luggage on the airport sidewalk, I realized that my frustration had only just begun.

2   This was my first visit to the international terminal of the airport, and nothing was familiar. I could not make sense of any of the signs. Where was the check-in counter? Where should I take my luggage? I had no idea where the immigration line was. I began to panic. What time was it? Where was my plane? I had to find help because I could not be late!

3 I tried to ask a passing businessman for help, but my words all came out wrong. He just **scowled** and walked away. What had happened? I had been in this country for a whole semester, and I could not even remember how to ask for directions. This was awful! Another bus arrived at the **terminal**, and the passengers came out carrying all sorts of luggage. Here was my chance! I could follow them to the right place, and I would not have to say a word.

4 I dragged my enormous suitcase behind me and followed the group. We finally reached the elevators. Oh, no! They all fit in it, but there was not enough room for me. I watched in **despair** as the elevator doors closed. I had no idea what to do next. I got on the elevator when it returned and **gazed** at all the buttons. Which one could it be? I pressed button 3. The elevator slowly climbed up to the third floor and **jerked** to a stop. A high, squeaking noise announced the opening of the doors, and I looked around **timidly**.

5 Tears formed in my eyes as I saw the **deserted** lobby and realized that I would miss my plane. Just then an **elderly** airport employee **shuffled** around the corner. He saw that I was lost and asked if he could help. He gave me his handkerchief to dry my eyes as I related my **predicament**. He smiled kindly, and led me down a long hallway. We walked up some stairs, turned a corner, and, at last, there was customs! He led me past all the lines of people and pushed my luggage to the inspection counter.

6 When I turned to thank him for all his help, he was gone. I will never know that kind man's name, but I will always remember his unexpected **courtesy**. He helped me when I needed it the most. I can only hope that one day I will be able to do the same for another traveler who is suffering through a terrible journey.

to scowl: to frown

a terminal: an arrival and departure point for some forms of mass transportation

to despair: the condition of having no hope

to gaze: to look at slowly and steadily

to jerk: to move with an abrupt motion

timidly: hesitantly, shyly

deserted: empty

elderly: older; mature

to shuffle: to walk by sliding one's feet along the ground

a predicament: a troubling situation

a courtesy: a kind or polite action

Post-Reading

1. What is the narrative hook?_____

_____

2. Do you think the hook is effective? In other words, did it grab your attention? Why, or why not?

_____

_____

3. Where is the setting of this story?

_____

4. What is the theme, or the basic idea, of "Frustration at the Airport"?

_____

_____

5. Read the final sentences in Paragraphs 2, 3, 4, and 5. How does each one prepare the reader for the action to come?

_____

_____

6. What do you think the mood of the story is? What feeling or atmosphere does the writer create?

_____

_____

_____

7. List the characters in this essay.

_____

8. What verb tense is used in "Frustration at the Airport"?_____. Write five verbs that the writer uses._____

_____

9. This essay is arranged in chronological order. In a few words, describe what happens first, second, third, and so on.

_____

_____

_____

_____

10. Underline the transitional sentences.

11. Does the story end with a moral, prediction, or revelation? _____ Write the final sentence here.

_____

_____

Building Better Sentences: For further practice, go to Practice 8 on page 196 in Appendix 1.

ACTIVITY 3 **Outlining Practice**

Below is an outline for "Frustration at the Airport." Some of the information is missing. Reread the essay beginning on page 43 and complete the outline.

Title: _____

  I. Introduction (Paragraph 1)

    A. Hook: I had never been more anxious in my life. I had just spent the last three endless hours trying to get to the airport so that I could travel home.

    B. Thesis statement: _____

_____

 II. Body

    A. Paragraph 2 (Event 1) topic sentence: This was my first visit to the international terminal of the airport, and nothing was familiar.

       1. The signs were confusing.

       2. I began to panic.

       3. Transition sentence: _____

_____

    B. Paragraph 3 (Event 2) topic sentence: _____

_____

       1. He scowled and walked away.

       2. I could not remember how to ask for directions.

       3. _____

       4. Transition sentence: _____

_____

SUPPORT

SUPPORT

C. Paragraph 4 (Event 3) topic sentence: I dragged my enormous suitcase behind me and followed the group.

    1. _____

    2. I got on the elevator and looked at the buttons.

    3. _____

    4. Transition sentence: _____

    _____

D. Paragraph 5 (Event 4) topic sentence: Tears formed in my eyes as I saw the deserted lobby and realized that I would miss my airplane.

    1. An airport employee offered to help.

    2. _____

    3. _____

    4. Transition sentence: He led me past all the lines of people and pushed my luggage to the inspection counter.

III. Conclusion (Paragraph 6)

    A. Close of the action: _____

    B. I will never know his name, but I will always remember his unexpected courtesy.

    C. _____

    D. Final sentence (moral, prediction, or revelation): _____

    _____

The following narrative essay is missing large parts of the story (supporting information in the body). As you read, add information that moves the story along. Be sure to write transition sentences at the end of Paragraphs 2, 3, and 4. If you need more space, use a separate piece of paper.

Essay 9

A Bad Day

1   I should never have deleted the chain letter e-mail from my computer. The letter clearly warned me that if I did, I would have one day of bad luck. Unlike my mother, I tend not to believe these types of things bringing bad luck: breaking a mirror, someone giving me the "evil eye," or even opening an umbrella in the house. As a result, I got rid of this **superstitious** e-mail with one quick click of the mouse. That night, however, as I fell asleep, I had the uncomfortable feeling that something was not quite right.

superstitious:
irrational, believing in things that are not based on science

2   When I woke up the next morning, I was surprised to find that I had overslept and would be late for work. As I rushed down the stairs to eat a quick breakfast, I **tripped** over my bag and _____

to trip: to stumble or fall

_____

_____

_____

_____

_____

_____

_____

_____

3   On my way to work, I decided to take a shortcut through an old part of town.

_____

_____

_____

_____

_____

_____

_____

4   When I arrived at work, I found a note from my boss on my desk. She wanted to see me **right away**. I took a deep breath and walked into her office. As I stepped inside, I noticed a scowl on her face.

right away: immediately

_____

_____

_____

_____

_____

_____

_____

5   Finally, after a long and difficult day, I returned home to find that my air conditioner was broken. I could not take it anymore! It had been the worst day ever, and I did not want anything else to happen. I rushed to my computer, opened up my e-mail, and went directly to the deleted e-mail folder. I opened up the letter and reread the words: "Send ten copies of this e-mail to your friends, and you will have good luck for a year." I put on my reading glasses and began scrolling through my list of e-mail contacts. They could take their chances, but I was not going to have any more bad luck!

Building Better Sentences: For further practice, go to Practice 9 on page 197 in Appendix 1.

Grammar for Writing

Connectors and Time Relationship Words

The most common way to organize events in a narrative essay is in chronological order. The event that occurs first is in the introduction, and the events that follow are in the next paragraphs (the body) and continue to the end (the conclusion).

To make sure that readers understand time relationships, effective writers use connecting words and phrases to show how events progress. Look at the time words in the chart below. These are connectors that you can use in narrative writing.

Chronological Order	Prepositions	Time Words That Begin Clauses *
first (second, third, etc.)	after (a moment)	after
next	at (9:00 A.M.)	as soon as
finally	by (bedtime, then)	before
later	during (the afternoon)	until
now	from (then on)	when
then	until (five o'clock)	whenever
		while

*When time clauses occur at the beginning of a sentence, they MUST be followed by a comma.

Sentence Variety with Prepositions of Time Plus Key Nouns for Better Cohesion

Essays that are written using only one or two sentence patterns can be dull to read. Good writers try to include variety in their sentences. Here are two ways to add variety with time words.

1. Follow the time word *after* with a noun.

   Change Marta studied engineering at the University of Charleston. She graduated in 2013. Then she got a job with Johnson and Rowe, a local engineering firm.

   to Marta studied engineering at the University of Charleston. **After her graduation in 2013**, she got a job with Johnson and Rowe, a local engineering firm.

   Change I walked up the stairs to the stage. I was so frightened to begin my speech that I could actually hear my teeth chattering. I remembered my deep breathing exercise, looked confidently at my audience, and began to speak.

   to I walked up the stairs to the stage. I was so frightened to begin my speech that I could actually hear my teeth chattering. **After my deep breathing exercise**, I looked confidently at my audience and began to speak.

2. Follow *after, before, while,* and *when* with a gerund* (an -*ing* verb form used as a noun).

   Change A rare golden Sitka spruce was cut down by vandals. It had been growing for more than three hundred years.

   to **After growing** for more than three hundred years, a rare golden Sitka spruce was cut down by vandals.

   Change Joanna Cannon ran for mayor. She promised to lower property taxes.

   to **While running** for mayor, Joanna Cannon promised to lower property taxes.

*A gerund is a verb form that ends in -*ing* and is used as a noun, such as *walking* and *studying*.

For a more complete list of connectors, see the *Brief Writer's Handbook with Activities*, pages 180–181.

Read the essay. Fill in the blanks with an appropriate connector or time relationship word or phrase. Refer to the chart on page 50.

Essay 10

Becoming a Man

1   When they are asked who their **idol** is, most people will name a famous person. I am not most people. My idol is a person whom I have known my entire life. He is my brother Claudio, and even today he teaches me about life. The day that Claudio taught me the importance of being a man is the day he left home to go to college.

an idol: hero

2   It was an early Saturday morning in August. As usual, we were woken up by the sound of our sister playing the piano. She was always playing that **silly** instrument! _____ a few minutes of lying in our beds, wishing she would stop, we slowly got up. _____ that point, we knew we could not fall back asleep. She was probably going to play that piano all day!

silly: stupid, ridiculous

3   _____ we reached the kitchen, there was a surprise for Claudio—his favorite breakfast. _____ Mom saw us, she gave us a big smile and told us to sit down for our pancakes. It was obvious that this was an important day for everyone. _____ we were finishing breakfast, Claudio went upstairs to continue **packing**.

to pack: to put clothes in a suitcase

4 _____ I heard him call my name, I ran to the room we shared, sat down on the bed, and watched Claudio close his suitcase. He turned to me and nodded. "It's time, brother," he said. I thought he was referring to his time to leave the house. Actually, he went on to explain all of the important responsibilities that I would have after he was gone. Claudio meant that it was time for me **to take on** a bigger role in the family. _____ that point, I understood everything.

to take on: undertake, face

5 _____ then on, I took my **role** as the "man of the house" very seriously. With Claudio away, I would need to be available for Mom whenever she needed me. What have I learned from my brother? I have learned about family, love, and responsibility.

a role: job, function

> **Building Better Sentences**: For further practice, go to Practice 10 on page 198 in Appendix 1.

Grammar for Writing

Adjective Clauses

Adjective clauses are one of the most powerful ways to combine two ideas (simple sentences) into one complex sentence. Study the following rules and examples:

1. Adjective clauses must contain a subject and a verb.

2. The subject of an adjective clause can be *who* (people), *which* (things), or *that* (people or things).

    Samir studies at a university. The university is well known for its technology programs.

    adjective clause
    Samir studies at a university <u>that is well known for its technology programs</u>.

3. If the information in the adjective clause is necessary to clarify the person or thing you are writing about, do not use a comma to separate the ideas. However, if the information in the adjective clause is not necessary to understand the meaning of the sentence, use a comma, or pair of commas, to separate the adjective clause from the rest of the sentence. In other words, commas indicate the information is extra. Study the examples below.

Necessary Information	Unnecessary Information
The city **that we will visit last on our trip** is located in central Florida.	Orlando, **which we will visit last on our trip**, is located in central Florida.
NOTE: When the writer says *the city,* it is not clear which city the writer is talking about. The adjective clause *(that we will visit last on our trip)* is important information for readers because it tells them which city in central Florida the writer is referring to.	**NOTE:** When the writer says *Orlando,* the readers know which city the writer is talking about. The information about when the writer will visit this city does not affect our ability to know that the writer is referring to Orlando.

Read the following narrative essay. Find and underline the nine adjective clauses in the essay. Hint: Adjective clauses tend to begin with *who*, *that*, or *which*.

Essay 11

Learning to Drive

1   I could not believe it. Driving laws in Ontario allowed teenagers to get their licenses at the age of sixteen! As my sixteenth birthday approached, I beamed with excitement and anticipation. What I did not know at the time was this: The driving lessons that I learned in our old sedan would stay with me for the rest of my life.

2   My father, who adored driving, was the obvious choice to be my driving instructor. The first lesson took place in the **driveway**. While I sat in the passenger seat, he explained the devices in the car. I was particularly frightened by the gear shift, which was sticking out of the floorboard. However, my father patiently lectured on the different floor pedals, the turn signals, and, my favorite, the car horn.

3   For the next lesson, I sat in the driver's seat. At that time, it felt more like a **throne** than anything else. My father asked me to turn on the car, and then he guided me into reverse. As I let up on the clutch and pressed the gas, I felt the car starting to move backward. I was controlling this vehicle! Slowly and carefully, I backed out of the driveway and into the **residential** street. After a few moments of confusion, I had the car sputtering forward in first gear.

a driveway: an area in front of a home where people park their cars

a throne: a special chair meant for nobility

residential: areas where people live, not commercial

4   Two weeks of lessons passed, and I was beginning to get bored with the scenery, which never changed. My father had me drive around the same block again and again. I was passing the same landmarks—the neighbors' houses, the dead tree down the street, and the kids who were playing in the empty lot on the corner. When I could stand it no more, I asked to move to a street that had more action. "Tomorrow. I think you are ready," my father replied, his eyes twinkling with pride.

5   My emotions were in overdrive the next day. I was finally on a busy street at night. I shifted from first gear to second gear with no problems. Then came third gear. When I reached the speed that I wanted, I put the car into fourth. I was flying in the old **sedan**! My father's concerned voice broke my **spell**. He said calmly, "Honey, there's a red light ahead." I was traveling far above the speed limit and heading toward a red light. All the information that I had learned in the previous weeks **leaked out** of my brain. I did not know how to react. I blared the horn and flew through the intersection, which by pure luck was empty.

6   That night my father was **somber**. I was in tears. How lucky we had been not to have been hit by another car. I waited for him to **reprimand** me, but he did not. I was aware of the **severity** of my **moving violation**. It is now thirty years later, and I have not forgotten that day. In fact, if I accidentally drive through a red light now, I remember the emotions of a sixteen-year-old and the wisdom of a loving father who taught her to drive.

a sedan: a type of car

a spell: a state of being captivated by something

to leak out: escape from one's memory

somber: serious

to reprimand: scold; lecture

severity: seriousness

a moving violation: a traffic offense

Building Better Sentences: For further practice, go to Practice 11 on page 199 in Appendix 1.

Building Better Vocabulary

ACTIVITY 7   **Word Associations**

Circle the word or phrase that is most closely related to the word or phrase on the left. If necessary, use a dictionary to check the meaning of words you do not know.

	A	B
1. a scowl	a happy face	an angry face
2. a predicament	good luck	trouble
3. to shuffle	ears	feet
4. to gaze	eyes	mouth
5. knowledge	a lot of information	almost no information
6. idol	celebrity	violation
7. somber	serious	understanding

8. residential*	houses and apartments	offices
9. driveway	cars	people
10. severity	funny	serious

*Indicates words that are part of the Academic Word List. See pages 183–184 for a complete list.

ACTIVITY 8 Using Collocations

Fill in each blank with the word or phrase on the left that most naturally completes the phrase on the right. If necessary, use a dictionary to check the meaning of words you do not know.

1. ask / to ask   how _____ for help

2. journey / lobby   a deserted _____

3. feeling / letter   an uncomfortable ___ _____

4. through / down   to rush _____ the stairs

5. from / by   hit _____ a car

6. by / on   to trip _____ something

7. do / make   to _____ _____ sense of something

8. bed / table   sit down on the _____

9. say / tell   to _____ the truth

10. lesson / street   learn a _____

Developing a Narrative Essay

   When writing a narrative essay there are a few strategies that can help you. These are choosing a topic, brainstorming, and making an outline.

Choosing a Topic

   When you write a narrative essay, choose a topic that is important to you—your essay will be easier to write and more interesting to read if you do. Also remember that smaller is better. The smaller the action or event you choose, the easier it will be to keep your readers' interest and describe the action fully. Choose a topic that you can write about in approximately five or six paragraphs. For example, it would be impossible to describe—in one essay—all the events that helped make you the person you are today. However, you could choose one event that made a difference in your life, such as your first job or a special award, and write an essay about that. At the same time, be careful that the topic you choose is not too small. For example, a story about how your little brother called you a name one day would not be a good topic for a narrative essay. There needs to be enough action to make a story of five or six paragraphs.

Ask Yourself Questions

To help you think of some possible topics for narrative essays, ask yourself questions. Use the following questions as a guide:

- When was an important time in my life? Remember, the experience can be a very short one, such as "July 13, 2013," in which the writer describes a five-minute segment of her life.

- What has happened in my experience that I would enjoy writing about?

- Is there an event in my life that other people (readers) would enjoy hearing about?

- How did I feel about a particular experience?

- Who was involved?

- Why do I remember this event so strongly? What effect did it have on me?

- Did anything change because of this experience?

- What interesting experiences do I know of that happened to other people?

If you are able to answer some of these questions about a specific experience that you or someone else had, then you may have a topic for a narrative essay.

ACTIVITY 9 **Choosing Topics**

Look at the pairs of topics. Put a ✓ next to the topic that is the better choice for a narrative essay.

1. _____ Your last year in high school

   _____ Your last day in high school

2. _____ A scary airplane ride to another city

   _____ A scary trip around the world

3. _____ Guidelines for buying a car

   _____ Buying your first car

4. _____ Important academic ceremonies that you have participated in

   _____ Your brother's embarrassing wedding ceremony

5. _____ What I did last New Year's Eve

   _____ What I did last year

ACTIVITY 10   Ideas for a Narrative Essay

Take a few minutes to think about possible topics for a narrative essay. Write some ideas here.

_____

_____

_____

Brainstorming

Brainstorming is a process to help you generate ideas about essay topics. When you brainstorm, do not worry about correct grammar or spelling. Just focus on getting your ideas on paper. Here are three ways to brainstorm ideas for an essay:

1. **Ask *wh-* questions about your topic.** With this method, you begin with a general idea of the topic that you are interested in. Then ask the questions *Who? What? When? Where? Why?* and, in some cases, *How?* The answers to these questions will help clarify what you would like to write about.

Here is an example:

General topic: *Celebrating Women's Day*

Questions: <u>Who</u> *celebrates Women's Day?* <u>What</u> *is the history of this celebration?* <u>When</u> *does the celebration take place? In* <u>what</u> *parts of the world is Women's Day celebrated?* <u>Why</u> *is it celebrated?* <u>How</u> *do people celebrate women on this day?* <u>How</u> *is it the same or different from Mother's Day?*

2. **Make a list of words or phrases that describe your topic.** This list can help with vocabulary choices when you write your essay. Here is a sample list on the topic of Women's Day. Remember, this is the first step in the writing process, so many of your ideas might change.

March	**flowers**	**my family**
gifts	**history**	**tradition**
respect	**candy**	**men give to women**

3. **Make a visual map of your essay ideas.** One kind of visual map is called **clustering**.

   To make a cluster map, write your topic in the center of a piece of paper and then circle it. Then draw lines out from the circle. At the end of those lines write words and ideas associated with the topic. Write whatever comes to mind. Connect any words that are related with lines. When you are finished, you will have many new ideas about your topic. Here is an example of clustering on the topic of Women's Day:

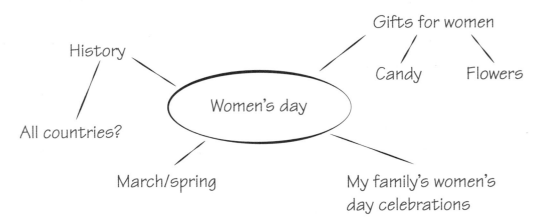

Original Student Writing: Narrative Essay

Developing Narrative Ideas

Follow the steps below to develop ideas for a narrative essay.

1. Choose a topic that is suitable for a narrative essay. You may want to look at your notes from Activity 10 to help you. Remember that in a narrative essay you tell a story. Work with other students to see if your topic is appropriate.

2. After you have a suitable topic, brainstorm some ideas about your topic. Use a separate piece of paper.

3. Now it is time to begin organizing your ideas. Remember that it is not necessary to tell every detail of the story. Include only the most important actions or events that move the story forward.

   a. Introduction (beginning of the story): theme, setting, and characters.

   What is the basic idea of the story? Where does the story take place? When does the story take place? Who is in the story?

   _____

   _____

   _____

   b. Body (middle of the story): mood and plot

   What feeling or atmosphere do you want to create in your story? What will happen in the story?

   _____

   _____

   _____

   c. Conclusion (end of the story): end of the action, moral, prediction, or revelation

   What will happen last in your story? How will you wrap up the action of the story? Will your narrative essay have a moral, make a prediction, or provide a revelation?

   _____

   _____

   _____

If you need ideas for words and phrases, see the Useful Vocabulary for Better Writing on pages 185–188.

ACTIVITY 12 **Planning with an Outline**

Use the outline on pages 60 and 61 as a guide to help you make a more detailed plan for your narrative essay. You may need to use either more or fewer points under each heading. Include your ideas from Activity 11. Where possible, write in complete sentences.

Topic: _____

I. Introduction (Paragraph 1)

    A. Hook: _____

    _____

    B. Connecting information: _____

    _____

    _____

    C. Thesis statement: _____

    _____

II. Body

    A. Paragraph 2 (Event 1) topic sentence: _____

    _____

    SUPPORT

        1. _____

        2. _____

        3. Transition sentence: _____

        _____

    B. Paragraph 3 (Event 2) topic sentence: _____

    _____

    SUPPORT

        1. _____

        2. _____

        3. Transition sentence: _____

        _____

    C. Paragraph 4 (Event 3) topic sentence: _____

    _____

    SUPPORT

        1. _____

        2. _____

        3. Transition sentence: _____

        _____

D. Paragraph 5 (Event 4) topic sentence: _____

_____

1. _____

2. _____

3. Transition sentence: _____

_____

III. Conclusion (Paragraph 6)

A. Close of the action: _____

_____

B. _____

_____

C. _____

_____

D. Final sentence (moral, prediction, or revelation): _____

_____

About Peer Editing

Think of the first draft of your essay as your first attempt. Before you rewrite it, it is helpful to ask someone to read your paper, offer comments, and ask questions about your essay. Many writers do not always see their weak areas, but a reader can help you see where you need to make improvements.

In class, peer editing is an easy way to get opinions on your essay. With this method, other students (your peers) read your essay and make comments using a set of questions and guidelines from the Peer Editing Sheets found on NGL.Cengage.com/GW4. You will read someone else's essay, too. Peer editing can help you improve any areas that are not strong or clear up any areas that seem confusing to the reader.

Writer's Note

Suggestions for Peer Editing

Listen carefully. In peer editing, you will receive many comments and some suggestions from other students. It is important to listen carefully to comments about your writing. You may think that what you wrote is clear and accurate, but readers can often point out places that need improvement. Don't be defensive. Remember that the comments are about the writing, not about you!

Make helpful comments. When you read your classmates' essays, choose your words and comments carefully so that you do not hurt their feelings. For example, instead of saying, "This is bad grammar," be more specific and say, "You need to make sure that every sentence has a verb." Instead of saying, "I cannot understand any of your ideas," write a more specific note such as, "What do you mean in this sentence?"

ACTIVITY 13 Peer Editing Your Outline

Exchange books with a partner and look at Activity 12. Read your partner's outline. Then use Peer Editing Sheet 1 on NGL.Cengage.com/GW4 to help you comment on your partner's outline. There is a sample Peer Editing Sheet in Appendix 2. Use your partner's feedback to revise your outline. Make sure you have enough information to develop your supporting sentences.

ACTIVITY 14 Writing a Narrative Essay

Write a narrative essay based on your revised outline from Activity 13. Use at least two of the vocabulary words or phrases presented in Activities 7 and 8. Underline these words and phrases in your essay. Be sure to refer to the seven steps in the writing process in the *Brief Writer's Handbook with Activities* on pages 156–163.

If you need ideas for words and phrases, see the Useful Vocabulary for Better Writing on pages 185–188.

ACTIVITY 15 Peer Editing Your Essay

Exchange papers from Activity 14 with a partner. Read your partner's essay. Then use Peer Editing Sheet 2 on NGL.Cengage.com/GW4 to help you comment on your partner's writing. Be sure to offer positive suggestions and comments that will help your partner improve his or her writing. Consider your partner's comments as you revise your own essay.

Additional Topics for Writing

Here are more ideas for topics for a narrative essay. Before you write, be sure to refer to the seven steps in the writing process in the *Brief Writer's Handbook with Activities*, pages 156–163.

**PHOTO
TOPIC:** Look at the photograph on pages 38–39. Write a story about a person who inspires you. What does this person do? Why is it important? How does this person influence you and others?

TOPIC 2: Think of a person that you know well. Be sure that you feel comfortable writing about him or her. Tell a story about this person. What unusual or exciting experience has this person had? How did he or she influence you?

TOPIC 3: Write about an important event in history from the point of view of someone who lived at that time.

TOPIC 4: Choose a piece of music and listen to it. When you hear the music, what do you imagine is happening? Create a story that describes what is happening in the music.

TOPIC 5: Think back to your childhood and a time when you were punished for doing something wrong. Write a narrative about that event, including what you did, who you were with, and how you were punished.

Timed Writing

How quickly can you write in English? There are many times when you must write quickly, such as on a test. It is important to feel comfortable during those times. Timed-writing practice can make you feel better about writing quickly in English.

1. Take out a piece of paper.

2. Read the essay guidelines and the writing prompt.

3. Write a basic outline, including the thesis and your three main points.

4. Write a five-paragraph essay.

5. You have 40 minutes to write your essay.

Narrative Essay Guidelines

- Remember to give your essay a title.

- Double-space your essay.

- Write as legibly as possible (if you are not using a computer).

- Select an appropriate principle of organization for your topic.

- Include a short introduction that serves as background information, three body paragraphs that tell the narrative, and an appropriate conclusion.

- Try to give yourself a few minutes before the end of the activity to review your work. Check for spelling, verb tense, and subject-verb agreement mistakes.

Narrate a story about a disagreement you had with a friend (or family member) and how the disagreement was resolved.

In Nunavut, Canada, a sledder holds a photograph of a South Carolina swamp to show how different the Arctic looked 56 million years ago.

Can you compare or contrast two places on earth?

What Is a Comparison Essay?

In a **comparison essay**, you can compare ideas, people, different times in history, or other things. The subjects of this kind of essay are two items that are related in some way. You can focus on the similarities between the two items, on the differences, or on both the similarities and the differences. Your goal is to show your readers how these items are similar or different, what their strengths and weaknesses are, or what their advantages and disadvantages are. In a history class, your essay might compare the French Revolution and the American Revolution. In an economics class, you might write about the similarities and differences between capitalism and socialism. In an art class, you might write about the differences in the works of two impressionist painters, such as Monet and Renoir.

Like other essays, the comparison essay has an introductory paragraph that contains a hook and a thesis statement, two or three or more paragraphs that make up the body, and a concluding paragraph.

Girl with a Fan by Pierre-Auguste Renoir

Banks of the Seine, Vétheuil, by Claude Oscar Monet

Patterns of Organization

There are two basic ways to organize a comparison essay—the block method and the point-by-point method.

Block Method	Point-by-Point Method
With the **block method**, you present one subject and all its points of comparison; then you do the same for the second subject. With this organization, you discuss each subject completely without interruption.	With the **point-by-point method**, you include both subjects in one point of comparison before moving on to the next point of comparison.
Introduction: Hook + thesis (Paragraph 1) **Body:** Supporting Information **Paragraph 2:** Renoir's inspirations, painting style, and most famous works. **Paragraph 3:** Monet's inspirations, painting style, and most famous works. **Conclusion:** Conclusion (restated information + suggestion or opinion) (Paragraph 4)	**Introduction:** Hook + thesis (Paragraph 1) **Body:** Supporting Information **Paragraph 2:** artistic inspirations (of Renoir and Monet) **Paragraph 3:** painting styles (of Renoir and Monet) **Paragraph 4:** Most famous works (of Renoir and Monet) **Conclusion:** (restated information + suggestion or opinion) (Paragraph 5)

Parallel Organization of Supporting Information

In the block-method example, notice that the supporting information in Paragraph 2 includes inspirations, painting style, and most famous works. The supporting information in Paragraph 3 also includes these three aspects of the artist. In the point-by-point method, the supporting information includes inspirations, painting style, and most famous works as well, but information about both artists is presented in one setting before going on to discuss both artists in the next setting.

These repeated structures are called parallel organization. No matter which overall method of organization you choose, parallel organization is required of your information in all comparison essays.

Choosing a Method of Organization

Review the two methods of organizing a compare-contrast essay and answer the questions.

1. What are the advantages of the block method for the writer? For the reader?

2. What are the advantages of the point-by-point method for the writer? For the reader?

ACTIVITY 1 **Studying a Comparison Essay**

This essay compares some features of Brazil and the United States. Discuss the Preview Questions with a partner. Then read the essay and answer the questions that follow.

Preview Questions

1. What do you know about the different cultural groups who live in Brazil and the United States?

2. What does the word *individualism* mean to you?

Essay 12

Not as Different as One Would Think

1   All countries in the world are unique. Obviously, countries are different from one another in location, size, culture, government, climate, and lifestyle. However, many countries share some surprising similarities. Some may think that these two nations have nothing in common because Brazil and the United States are in different **hemispheres**. On the contrary, they share many similarities.

a hemisphere: one half of the world

2   One important similarity is their size. Both Brazil and the United States are large countries. Brazil covers almost half of the South American continent. Few Brazilians can say that they have traveled **extensively** within the country's borders. Because Brazil covers such a large geographic area, its weather varies greatly from one area to another. Like Brazil, the United States takes up a significant portion of its continent (North America), so most Americans have visited only a few of the 50 states. In addition, the United States has a wide range of **climates**. When the Northeast is experiencing snowstorms, cities like Miami, Florida, can have temperatures over 85 degrees Fahrenheit.

extensively: widely, over a large area

the climate: the usual weather of a region

3   Another similarity between Brazil and the United States is the **diversity** of ethnic groups. Brazil was colonized by Europeans, and its culture has been greatly influenced by this fact. However, the identity of the Brazilian people is not **solely** a product of Western civilization. Brazil is a "melting pot" of many ethnic groups that immigrated there and mixed with the **indigenous** people. The United States also has a diversity of ethnic groups representing the early colonists from northern Europe as well as groups from Africa, the Mediterranean, Asia, and South America. The mixture of cultures and **customs** has worked to form ethnically rich cultures in both countries.

diversity: variety

solely: exclusively

indigenous: native, original

a custom: a learned social or cultural behavior

4   Finally, **individualism** is an important value for both Brazilians and Americans. Brazil works hard to defend the **concept** of freedom of choice. Citizens believe that they have the right to do and be whatever they desire as long as they do not hurt others. Individualism and freedom of choice also exist in the United States, where freedom is perhaps the highest value of the people. Some people may believe that the desire for individual expression is divisive and can make a country weak. However, the ability of people to be whatever they want makes both countries strong.

individualism: uniqueness, independence

a concept: an idea

5   Although Brazil and the United States are unique countries, there are **remarkable** similarities in their size, ethnic diversity, and personal values. Some people tend to believe that their culture and country are without equal. Nevertheless, it is important to remember that people as a whole have more in common than they generally think they do.

remarkable: amazing, extraordinary

Post-Reading

1. What two subjects does the writer compare in this essay?

_____

2. What method of organization does the writer use—point-by-point or block?

_____

3. What is the hook for this essay? Write it here.

_____

_____

_____

4. Underline the thesis statement. Is the thesis restated in the conclusion (Paragraph 5)? If yes, underline the sentence in the conclusion that restates the thesis.

5. In Paragraph 2, the author writes about the ways in which size affects Brazil and the United States. In the following chart, list the supporting information the writer uses.

The Effects of Size	
Brazil	United States
a. _____ _____	a. _____ _____
b. _____ _____	b. _____ _____
c. _____ _____	c. _____ _____

6. Reread the concluding paragraph of "Not as Different as One Might Think." Does the writer offer a suggestion, an opinion, or a prediction? _____ Write the concluding sentence here.

_____

_____

Building Better Sentences: For further practice, go to Practice 12 on page 199 in Appendix 1.

Developing a Comparison Essay

In this next section, you will develop a comparison essay as you make an outline, write supporting information, and study connectors.

ACTIVITY 2 Outlining Practice

Below is a specific outline for "Not as Different as One Might Think." Some of the information is missing. Reread the essay beginning on page 68 and complete the outline.

Title: _____

I. Introduction (Paragraph 1)

    A. Hook: _All countries in the world are unique._____

    B. Connecting information: Different location, size, culture, government, climate, lifestyle

    C. Thesis statement: _____

    _____

II. Body

A. Paragraph 2 (Similarity 1) topic sentence: _____

_____

SUPPORT

   1. Brazil's characteristics

      a. Size: _____

      b. Travel: Few Brazilians have traveled extensively in their country.

      c. Climate: _____

   2. _____

      a. _____

      b. Travel: _____

      c. Climate: The weather can be extremely different in the northern and the southern parts of the country.

B. Paragraph 3 (Similarity 2) topic sentence: Another similarity is the diversity of ethnic groups.

   1. Brazil

      a. _____

      b. Other ethnic groups

      c. _____

SUPPORT

   2. United States

      a. Europe

      b. Africa

      c. the Mediterranean

      d. _____

      e. _____

C. Paragraph 4 (Similarity 3) topic sentence: _____

_____

SUPPORT

   1. Brazilians' belief in freedom: _____

_____

   2. _____

_____

III. Conclusion (Paragraph 5)

    A. Restated thesis: _____

    _____

    B. Opinion: Nevertheless, it is important to remember that people as a whole have more in common than they generally think they do.

ACTIVITY 3   **Supporting Information**

The following comparison essay is missing the supporting information. Work with a partner to write supporting sentences for each paragraph. If you need more space, use a separate piece of paper. After you finish, compare your supporting information with that of other students. (Note: This essay follows the point-by-point organizational pattern.)

Essay 13

On the Desk or on the Lap?

1   Some years ago, buying a computer was considered by many to be a very frightening task. For one, personal computing was advanced technology that was being advertised to the general public for the first time. These computers were also extremely expensive, and to tell the truth, many consumers did not know whether these devices would one day be considered just a fad. History, of course, has shown that computers are here to stay. Computer technology has exceeded most people's expectations. Still, even today, computer shoppers need to know what their options are. One of the biggest considerations for a computer purchase is "desktop or laptop?" To reach a decision, a buyer can compare these two computer types in terms of their overall cost, convenience, and style.

2   Desktop computers and laptops differ in their costs. _____

_____

_____

_____

_____

_____

_____

_____

3   Another thing to consider is the convenience factor. _____

_____

_____

_____

_____

_____

_____

_____

4   Finally, there is the subject of style. _____

_____

_____

_____

_____

_____

_____

_____

5 Choosing between a desktop model and a laptop is a personal decision for the consumer. This decision can be made more easily by looking at the cost, convenience, and style preferences. While it can seem like a daunting task now, it will certainly become more and more difficult as new "species" of computers come on the market.

Building Better Sentences: For further practice, go to Practice 13 on page 200 in Appendix 1.

Writer's Note

Asking Questions

How can you develop details and facts that will support your main ideas (topic sentences) in each paragraph? One of the best ways to write this supporting information is to ask yourself questions about the topic—*Where? Why? When? Who? What? How?*

Grammar for Writing

Sentence Structure of Connectors (for Comparison Essays)

Writers use **connectors** to help clarify their main ideas. Connectors help readers by providing logical connections between sentences, ideas, and paragraphs. Notice that when these words, and often the phrase that follows them, begin a sentence, they are followed by a comma.

Connectors That Show Comparison Between Sentences of Paragraphs

Between Sentences of Paragraphs	Examples
In addition, Subject + Verb.	Both Red Beauty and Midnight Dream roses are known for the size of their blooms, their color, and their fragrance. **In addition**, they are easy to grow.
Similarly, Subject + Verb.	The Midnight Dream rose won awards in local contests last year. **Similarly**, the Red Beauty rose was singled out for its beauty.
Likewise, Subject + Verb.	The blooms of Red Beauty roses last longer than those of most other roses. **Likewise**, the blooms of the Midnight Dream rose are long lasting.
Compared to ... , Subject + Verb.	Some roses last for a very short time. **Compared to** these roses, the blooms of Red Beauty and Midnight Dream roses last a long time.

Connectors That Show Contrast Between Sentences of Paragraphs

Between Sentences of Paragraphs	Examples
However, Subject + Verb. *or* **On the other hand**, Subject + Verb.	Many differences are clear to even novice gardeners. **However / On the other hand**, some of their differences are not very obvious.
In contrast, Subject + Verb.	Red Beauty has a strong, sweet fragrance. **In contrast**, Midnight Dream's fragrance is light and fruity.
Although Subject + Verb, Subject + Verb.	Both Midnight Dream roses and Red Beauty roses are red. **Although** both varieties produce red flowers, Midnight Dream roses are much darker than Red Beauty roses.
Even though Subject + Verb, Subject + Verb.	Red Beauty roses and Midnight Dream roses are long-stemmed roses. **Even though** both of these species are long stemmed, Red Beauty stems are thin and covered with thorns while Midnight Dream stems are thick and have almost no thorns.
Unlike Noun, Subject + Verb.	What do we know about the cost of these two kinds of roses? **Unlike** Red Beauty, Midnight Dream roses are relatively inexpensive.

For a more complete list of connectors, see the *Brief Writer's Handbook with Activities*, pages 180–181.

Read the following student essay and circle the appropriate connector in each set of parentheses. Refer to the charts on page 75 if necessary.

The writer in this essay uses the block method of writing to compare two parenting styles.

Essay 14

Parenting 101

1   The film previews are finished, and the movie theater is quiet as everyone waits for the feature film to appear. (1. However / On the other hand), the **stillness** is suddenly broken by a noise. The audience hears a sniffle. The sniffle soon turns to a cry, then a wail. There is an uncomfortable, or perhaps unhappy, toddler sitting in the movie theater. People start shuffling uncomfortably in their seats as they wait for what will happen next. Will the child be taken out of the theater, or will the parent pretend that everything is ok? **Scenarios** like these happen regularly. **Bystanders** wonder what the parent or caretaker will do. The action, of course, often depends on the type of parenting styles that adults use with their children. The two **extremes** are the **lenient (laissez-faire)** parent and the strict disciplinarian parent.

2   Lenient parents often focus on their child's having fun and enjoying "being a kid." If a child does something careless like break a glass, lenient parents will not become angry or scream. They know that the child is probably experimenting and meant no harm. (2. Likewise / Otherwise), they may even explain to the child that it was an accident and the child should not be upset or cry. (3. In contrast / In addition), lenient parents may not be too concerned about time-based activities and schedules. They will allow their children to stay up late and experience new things. The motto "You're only a kid once!" rings very true to these free spirits. This

a stillness: silence; tranquility

a scenario: situation

a bystander: people who witness something but are not involved

an extreme: boundaries, opposites

lenient: easy-going; relaxed

laissez-faire: (French) "let it be" or "leave it alone"

type of parent sees themselves as guides for their children, which cannot be said about the second parenting group: the disciplinarians.

3   Disciplinarian parents consider themselves role models for their children. (4. Unlike / Similarly) laissez-faire parents, their main priorities are safety and protection of their children. In essence, children are **monitored** very carefully and may not be allowed to play outside, interact with animals, or rough-house in general. A child who experiences a strict upbringing may be encouraged to focus on his studies instead of making friends. (5. In addition / However), interaction may be limited to only close family members. Children who are raised in highly-disciplined environments are **poised** to do very well in school.

to monitor: observe, supervise

to be poised to: prepared to

4   In the end, no parents are truly 100 percent lenient or 100 percent strict when it comes to raising their child. Most fall somewhere in the middle depending on the child, the environment, and the particular situation. Society knows that both **child-rearing** styles have advantages and disadvantages, but the more interesting question is this: Which style will these children choose when the time comes for them to become parents?

child rearing: raising children, bringing up children

Building Better Sentences: For further practice, go to Practice 14 on page 201 in Appendix 1.

Building Better Vocabulary

ACTIVITY 5 **Word Associations**

Circle the word or phrase that is most closely related to the word or phrase on the left. If necessary, use a dictionary to check the meaning of words you do not know.

	A	B
1. diversity*	difference	distance
2. customs	shirts	traditions
3. a concept*	an idea	a traditional song
4. remarkable	amazing	repetitive
5. a hemisphere	in geography class	in math class
6. to rough-house	aggressive play	gentle play
7. monitor*	create	observe
8. disciplinarian	lenient	strict
9. likewise*	also	but
10. a climate	salary	weather

*Indicates words that are part of the Academic Word List. See pages 183–184 for a complete list.

ACTIVITY 6 **Using Collocations**

Fill in each blank with the word on the left that most naturally completes the phrase on the right. If necessary, use a dictionary to check the meaning of words you do not know.

1. make / pay   to _____ attention to something

2. task / way   a frightening _____

3. say / tell   to _____ the truth

4. find / reach   to _____ a decision

5. between / from   the differences _____ the two cities

6. personal / private   make a _____ decision

7. said / shown   history has _____

8. likewise / significant   a _____ portion

9. common / contrary   to have nothing in _____

10. crowds / groups   ethnic _____

Grammar for Writing

Using Adverb Clauses

Good writers use different types of sentences in their work, and sentence variety is certainly an important element in academic writing.

An adverb clause is a clause that indicates condition, contrast, reason, purpose, result, or a time relationship. An adverb clause begins with a connector called a subordinating conjunction. Examples of subordinating conjunctions are *if, although, after, since,* and *because.*

In the following sentences from essays in this book, the subordination conjunctions are circled and the adverb clauses are underlined.

(**Although**) Brazil and the United States are unique countries, there are remarkable similarities in their size, ethnic diversity, and personal values.

(**While**) it can seem like a daunting task now, it will certainly become more and more difficult as new "species" of computers come on the market.

(**When**) the Northeast is experiencing snowstorms, cities like Miami, Florida, can have temperatures over 85 degrees Fahrenheit.

(**If**) a child does something careless like break a glass, lenient parents will not become angry or scream.

Function	Subordinating Conjunctions (begin dependent clauses)	Transitions (usually precede independent clauses)
Concession	although even though though	Admittedly, Despite this, Even so, Nevertheless,
Contrast	although even though while	Conversely, In contrast, Instead, However, On the other hand,
Result	so so that	As a consequence, As a result, Consequently, Therefore, Thus,
Time Relationships	after as as soon as before until when whenever while	First, Second, Next, In the meantime, Meanwhile, Then, Finally, Subsequently, Afterward,
Cause / Reason	because since	
Condition	even if if provided that unless when	
Purpose	in order that so that	
Comparison		In the same way, Likewise, Similarly,
Examples		For example, In particular, Specifically, To illustrate,
Information		Furthermore, In addition, Moreover,
Refutation		On the contrary,

Identifying Adverb Clauses and Subordinating Conjunctions

Underline the six adverb clauses in these sentences from essays in this book. Circle the subordinating conjunctions. If a sentence does not have an adverb clause, write X on the line.

_____ 1. Unlike Red Beauty, Midnight Dream roses are relatively inexpensive.

_____ 2. When the Northeast is experiencing snowstorms, cities like Miami, Florida, can have temperatures over 85 degrees Fahrenheit.

_____ 3. Some may think that these two nations have nothing in common because Brazil and the United States are in different hemispheres.

_____ 4. Few Brazilians can say that they have traveled extensively within the country's borders.

_____ 5. Even though both of these species are long-stemmed, Red Beauty stems are thin and covered with thorns.

_____ 6. In contrast, lenient parents may not be too concerned about time-based activities and schedules.

_____ 7. If a child does something careless like break a glass, lenient parents will not become angry or scream.

_____ 8. People start shuffling uncomfortably in their seats as they wait for what will happen next.

_____ 9. Because Brazil covers such a large geographic area, its weather varies greatly from one area to another.

_____ 10. Nevertheless, it is important to remember that people as a whole have more in common than they generally think they do.

Developing Ideas for Writing

Brainstorming

You will be asked to write comparison essays in many of your classes. Often, you will be given the two subjects to be compared, such as two poems from a literature course, two political beliefs from a political science course, or an invention and a discovery from a history or science course. When you have to choose your own subjects for comparison, the following brainstorming tips will help you.

Tips for Brainstorming Subjects

1. **The subjects should have something in common.** For example, soccer and hockey are both fast-paced games that require a player to score a point by putting an object into a goal guarded by a player from the other team.
2. **The two subjects must also have some differences.** For example, the most obvious differences between the two games are the playing field, the protective equipment, and the number of players.
3. **You need to have enough information on each topic to make your comparisons.** If you choose two sports that are not well-known, it might be more difficult to find information about them.

Make a List

A good way to determine whether you have enough information about similarities and differences between two subjects is to brainstorm a list. Read the information in the lists below.

Ice Hockey	Soccer
played on ice	played on a grass field
six players on a team	11 players on a team
uses a puck	uses a soccer ball
(very popular sport)	(very popular sport)
(players use lots of protective pads)	(players use some protective pads)
(cannot touch the puck with your hands)	(cannot touch the ball with your hands)
(goal = puck in the net)	(goal = ball in the net)

As you can see, soccer and hockey have many similarities and a few differences. Notice that the similarities are circled. These are "links" between the two subjects. A writer could use these links to highlight the similarities between the two games or to lead into a discussion of the differences between them· "Although both soccer and hockey are popular, more schools have organized soccer teams than hockey. . . ."

Make a Venn Diagram

Another way to brainstorm similarities and differences is to use a Venn diagram. A Venn diagram is a visual representation of the similarities and differences between two concepts. Here is a Venn diagram of the characteristics of hockey and soccer.

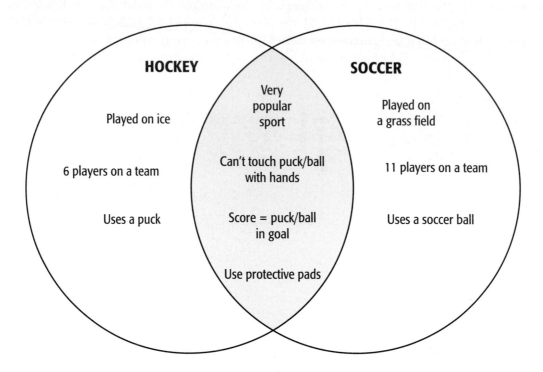

HOCKEY

Played on ice

6 players on a team

Uses a puck

Very popular sport

Can't touch puck/ball with hands

Score = puck/ball in goal

Use protective pads

SOCCER

Played on a grass field

11 players on a team

Uses a soccer ball

ACTIVITY 8 **Identifying Good Topics for a Comparison Essay**

Below are pairs of potential subjects for a comparison essay. Write *yes* on the line under the pairs that would be good topics and explain briefly what characteristics could be compared. Write *no* under the topics that would not be good choices and change one or both of them into more suitable topics. The first two have been done for you.

1. living in a house / living in an apartment

_yes—compare costs, privacy, space_____

2. international travel / domestic travel

_____

3. high school / college

_____

4. the weather in Toronto / tourist attractions in Toronto

_____

5. wild animals / animals in a zoo

_____

6. computers / computer keyboards

_____

7. hands / feet

_____

8. the surface of the ocean floor / the surface of the continents

_____

9. the Earth / the North American continent

_____

10. Chinese food / Mexican food

_____

Original Student Writing: Comparison Essay

ACTIVITY 9 **Working with a Topic**

Complete the following steps to develop ideas for a comparison essay.

1. Choose one topic from the list below or use your own idea for a topic. If you want to use an original idea, talk to your teacher to see if it is appropriate for a comparison essay.

two sports	two movies	two systems of education
two places	two machines	two kinds of professions
two desserts	two famous people	two celebrations or holidays

2. Use the following chart to brainstorm a list of information about each subject. If you like, use the list about soccer and hockey on page 81 as a guide.

TOPIC: _____	
Subject 1: _____	Subject 2: _____
_____	_____
_____	_____
_____	_____
_____	_____
_____	_____
_____	_____
_____	_____
_____	_____
_____	_____
_____	_____

3. Now fill in the Venn diagram using the information from the chart in Item 2 on page 83.

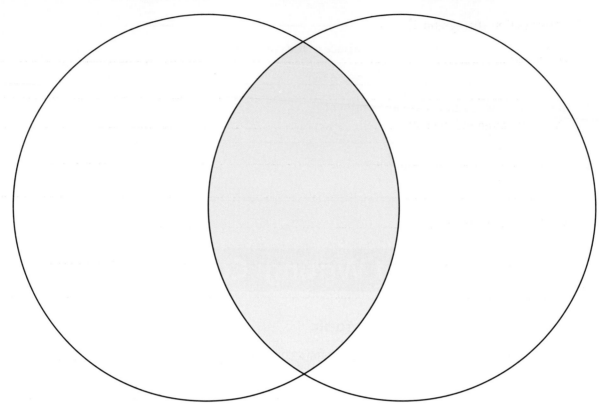

4. Decide if you are going to focus on the similarities or the differences between the two subjects or both in your comparison essay. Then choose three or four main points of comparison that you will use and list them here.

a. _____

b. _____

c. _____

d. _____

Writer's Note

Ideas for Supporting Information

In the next activity, you will develop supporting information. Here are some ideas to use as supporting information in your body paragraphs:

- give descriptions
- give examples
- explain the causes
- explain the effects

ACTIVITY 10 **Planning with an Outline**

Use the following outline to help you brainstorm a more detailed plan for your comparison essay. For this activity, use the point-by-point method of organization. Remember that the point-by-point method organizes each paragraph by one point of comparison, such as the languages, the populations, or the climates of two countries. Include your ideas from Activity 9. Write complete sentences where possible.

Topic: _____

I. Introduction (Paragraph 1)

   A. Hook: _____

      _____

   B. Connecting information: _____

      _____

      _____

   C. Thesis statement: _____

      _____

      _____

II. Body

   A. Paragraph 2 (first point of comparison) topic sentence: _____

      _____

      1. _____

         a. _____

         b. _____

      2. _____

         a. _____

         b. _____

SUPPORT

   B. Paragraph 3 (second point of comparison) topic sentence: _____

      _____

      1. _____

         a. _____

         b. _____

      2. _____

         a. _____

         b. _____

SUPPORT

C. Paragraph 4 (third point of comparison) topic sentence: _____

_____

SUPPORT

    1. _____

        a. _____

        b. _____

    2. _____

        a. _____

        b. _____

III. Conclusion (Paragraph 5)

    A. Restated thesis: _____

    B. Suggestion, opinion, or prediction:_____

> If you need ideas for words and phrases, see the Useful Vocabulary for Better Writing on pages 185–188.

ACTIVITY 11   Peer Editing Your Outline

Exchange books with a partner and look at Activity 10. Read your partner's outline. Then use Peer Editing Sheet 3 on NGL.Cengage.com/GW4 to help you comment on your partner's outline. Use your partner's feedback to revise your outline. Make sure you have enough information to develop your supporting sentences.

ACTIVITY 12   Writing a Comparison Essay

Write a comparison essay based on your revised outline from Activity 10. Use at least two of the vocabulary words or phrases presented in Activities 5 and 6. Underline these words and phrases in your essay. Be sure to refer to the seven steps in the writing process in the *Brief Writer's Handbook with Activities* on pages 156–163.

ACTIVITY 13   Peer Editing Your Essay

Exchange papers from Activity 12 with a partner. Read your partner's essay. Then use Peer Editing Sheet 4 on NGL.Cengage.com/GW4 to help you comment on your partner's writing. Be sure to offer positive suggestions and comments that will help your partner improve his or her essay. Consider your partner's comments as you revise your own essay.

Additional Topics for Writing

Here are more ideas for topics for a comparison essay. Before you write, be sure to refer to the seven steps in the writing process in the *Brief Writer's Handbook with Activities*, pages 156–163.

PHOTO
TOPIC: Look at the photograph on pages 64–65. Compare or contrast two places on Earth. How are these places alike or different? Have you been to these places? If not, how did you learn about them?

TOPIC 2: Compare the situation in a country before and after an important historical event, such as Cuba before and after Fidel Castro came to power.

TOPIC 3: Discuss two kinds of music, such as classical and pop. A few points of comparison might be artists, instruments, audiences, and popularity.

TOPIC 4: Show how the world has changed since the invention of the cell (mobile) phone. How did people communicate before its invention? How easy or difficult was it to get in contact with someone?

TOPIC 5: Show the similarities and differences in the ways that two cultures celebrate an important event, such as a birthday, wedding, or funeral.

Timed Writing

How quickly can you write in English? There are many times when you must write quickly such as on a test. It is important to feel comfortable during those times. Timed-writing practice can make you feel better about writing quickly in English.

1. Take out a piece of paper.

2. Read the essay guidelines and the writing prompt.

3. Write a basic outline, including the thesis and your three main points.

4. Write a five-paragraph essay.

5. You have 40 minutes to write your essay.

Comparison Essay Guidelines

- Use the point-by-point method.
- Remember to give your essay a title.
- Double-space your essay.
- Write as legibly as possible (if you are not using a computer).
- Select an appropriate principle of organization for your topic.
- Include a short introduction (with a thesis statement), three body paragraphs, and a conclusion.
- Try to give yourself a few minutes before the end of the activity to review your work. Check for spelling, verb tense, and subject-verb agreement mistakes.

Compare two popular vacation destinations.

Cause-Effect Essays

Severe storms caused the Gave de Pau river to overflow and destroy roads in Villelongue, France.

OBJECTIVES To learn how to write a cause-effect essay
To use connectors in cause-effect writing
To understand noun clauses

Can you write about some effects of extreme weather?

What Is a Cause-Effect Essay?

A **cause-effect essay** shows the reader the relationship between something that happens and its consequences, or between actions and results. For example, if too much commercial fishing is allowed in the North Atlantic Ocean (action), the fish population in some areas may diminish or disappear (result). Cause-effect essays can be informative, analytical, and insightful. In addition to being able to write a cause-effect essay, you need to know about this type of writing because you may want to include a single paragraph discussing a cause, an effect, or both in a longer essay you are writing, such as a persuasive or argumentative piece.

In this unit, you will study two kinds of cause-effect essays. Very simply, in one method, the writer focuses on the <u>causes</u> of something. Just think of how many people, when they are given a piece of information, like to analyze the topic and ask the question *Why?* or *How?* This is called the **focus-on-causes** method. In the second method, the writer emphasizes the <u>effects</u> or results of a cause. People who like to think hypothetically—answering the question *What if?*—focus on the outcome of a particular event or action. These writers often write **focus-on-effects** essays.

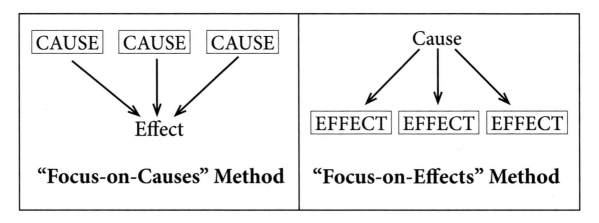

Imagine that your instructor gives you the following writing topic: quitting a job. You have the choice of using the focus-on-causes method or the focus-on-effects method.

Focus-on-causes method: You can choose to write an essay on why people quit their jobs and brainstorm possible reasons they may have for doing so, such as distance from the home or lack of benefits. Each paragraph would contain a different cause.

Focus-on-effects method: On the other hand, you may want to emphasize the effects of quitting a job—perhaps detailing the emotional and financial consequences—in your body paragraphs. In this case, each paragraph would address one effect.

These two cause-effect essay methods answer different questions. Essays that use the focus-on-causes method answer the question, **"Why does something happen?"** Essays that use the focus-on-effects method answer the question, **"What happens when…?"**

ACTIVITY 1 Studying a Cause-Effect Essay

This focus-on-causes essay answers the question, "Why do people lie?" Discuss the Preview Questions with a classmate. Then read the example essay and answer the questions that follow.

Preview Questions

1. Why do you think people lie?

2. Is it ever acceptable to lie? Give examples of acceptable and unacceptable lies.

The Truth Behind Lying

1   Most children are taught the virtue of honesty from fairy tales and other stories. The **celebrated** story of Pinocchio, who begins life as a **puppet**, teaches the importance of telling the truth. Every time Pinocchio lies, his nose grows longer and longer. Another story about the boy who "cried wolf" **exemplifies** how lying led to his losing all of his sheep as well as the trust of his fellow villagers. In the United States, young children learn the tale of young George Washington, who finally admits to his father that he cut down a cherry tree. These types of stories show children that "honesty is the best policy." Still, if this is the case, then why do so many people lie? The fact is that human beings lie for many reasons.

celebrated: famous, renowned

a puppet: a toy that is moved by strings

to exemplify: represent, typify

2   One reason for lying has to do with minimizing a mistake. While it is true that everyone makes a **blunder** from time to time, some people do not have the courage to admit their errors because they fear blame. For example, students might lie to their teachers about unfinished homework. They might say that they left the work at home when, in fact, they did not do the work at all. These students do not want to seem irresponsible, so they make up an excuse—a lie—to save face.

a blunder: a careless mistake

3   Another reason people lie is to get out of situations that they do not want to be in or cannot manage. For example, if a company decides to have a weekend meeting, one of the managers might not feel like attending. She may call her boss and give this excuse: "I've been fighting off a cold all week, and I truly cannot risk getting the others sick. I'll be sure to get all of the notes on Monday." When individuals do not want to admit the truth and then face the consequences, they use lies to **avoid** difficulties.

to avoid: to keep away from

4   In contrast, some people might tell a "white lie" when they do not want to hurt someone else's feelings. For example, if a good friend shows up with an **unflattering** new haircut, one could be truthful and say, "That haircut looks awful. What were you thinking?!" A more likely scenario is to say, "It's very original! It suits you," and spare the friend's feelings. These types of lies are generally not considered negative or wrong. In fact, many people who have told the truth to loved ones, only to see the negative reaction, wish they *had* told a white lie. Therefore, white lies can be useful in maintaining good relationships.

unflattering: unattractive, not favorable

5   A somewhat different reason for lying has to do with self-protection. Parents, particularly those with small children, may teach their children to use this type of "protective" lie in certain circumstances. What should children do if a stranger calls while the parents are out? Many parents teach their children to explain that mom and dad are too busy to come to the phone at that time. In this situation, protective lying can prevent harm or disaster.

6   People lie for many reasons, both good and bad. However, before people **resort to** lying in order to cover up mistakes or to avoid unpleasant situations, perhaps the motives for lying should be analyzed. One's lies may one day be exposed and cause severe embarrassment or the loss of people's trust.

to resort to: to do something only because other options have failed

Post-Reading

1. What is the thesis statement?_____

_____

2. What three examples of liars from famous stories does the author give in the introduction?

    a. _____

    b. _____

    c. _____

3   In Paragraph 4, the idiom *a white lie* is used in the topic sentence but is not defined. Write your own

    definition of a white lie. _____

_____

4. In Paragraph 5, the author supports the topic sentence by giving an example of a dangerous situation. What example does the author give?

_____

_____

5. Reread the concluding paragraph of "The Truth Behind Lying." Does the writer offer a suggestion, an opinion, or a prediction? _____ Write the final sentence here.

_____

_____

Building Better Sentences: For further practice, go to Practice 15 on page 202 in Appendix 1.

ACTIVITY 2 Studying a Focus-on-Effects Essay

This focus-on-effects essay discusses some of the effects of the breakup of the Soviet Union. Discuss the Preview Questions with a classmate. Then read the essay and answer the questions that follow.

1. What do you know about the Soviet Union? _____

2. Can you name any countries that were part of the Soviet Union?

_____

_____

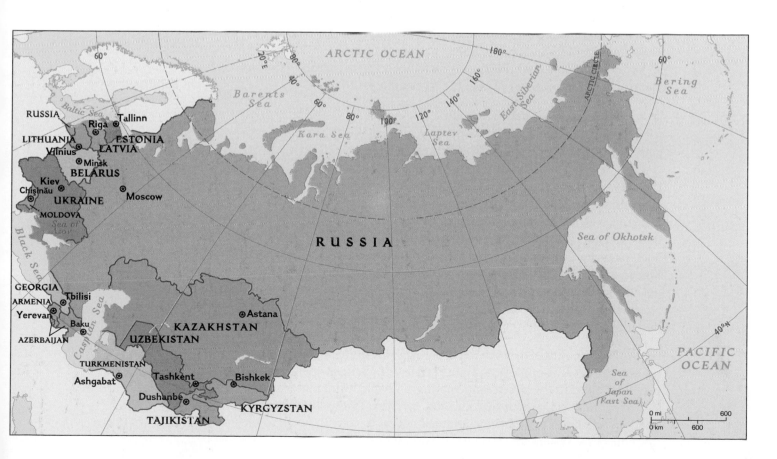

The Fall

1   For almost 50 years, the Cold War was one of the most talked about issues in international politics. Tensions between Western countries and the former Soviet Union were high, and the world felt the potential danger of a terrible conflict. When the Iron Curtain fell in 1991, many countries **rejoiced**. Independent-minded Soviet Republics got the independence they had wanted, and the communist **ideology** that had been so **prevalent** began to lose ground. Now, more than two decades after the breakup of the Soviet Union, the effects are still being felt.

2   One of the most obvious changes in post-communist **Eurasia** has been the **shift** to a market economy. Governments that once had **subsidized** the costs of basic necessities, such as food, transportation, housing, and electricity, are now letting competition and external factors determine the prices of these items. Inflation is high, and many citizens are having a difficult time adjusting to the **fluctuations** in prices based on supply and demand. However, imported goods are now commonplace in local markets, so consumers have more choices in what they buy. While the switch to a market economy is often a painful process, a majority of the citizens of the former Soviet Union are still confident that they will benefit financially from the economic changes.

3   Another anticipated effect of the fall of the Iron Curtain is **sovereignty**. The Soviet Union existed as one entity for many years, but many independent republics emerged, including Estonia, Latvia, Lithuania, Georgia, Ukraine, and Uzbekistan. These republics are currently in the process of shaping their own independent identities. They can focus on rebuilding their own cultures, languages, and priorities. This empowerment increases national pride and uniqueness. The idea of all Soviets being one and the same is certainly no more. Clearly, national identity is at the **forefront** of many people's minds.

4   While many former Soviets now feel a sense of national identity, the fall of the Soviet Union has taken away the identity of others. Many different ethnic groups have lived in this part of the world for generations. They were raised as Soviets, spoke Russian as a native language, and were taught to believe that they were citizens of the great superpower. Koreans, Tartars, Uighurs, and other ethnic groups can be found in most of the former Soviet Republics. Now that independence has spread from Eastern Europe to Central Asia, many of these citizens are considered minority groups. Where their ancestors are from does not matter to them as much as their current homeland. They may look Korean or Chinese, but most of them do not speak those languages and have not had ties with these parts of the world for many years. As the newly formed republics try to **reinvigorate** their traditions and values, many of the ethnic minorities tend to feel left out with no place to really call home.

5   The fall of the Soviet Union is perhaps one of the most **momentous** events of the last century. Walls fell, markets opened, and people rejoiced in the streets, anticipating a life filled with opportunities and freedom to make their own choices. A system that took so long to build will probably need as much time, if not more, to truly adapt to the free enterprise system that is now the world model.

---

to rejoice: to celebrate

an ideology: a system of beliefs

prevalent: common, accepted

Eurasia: the area of Europe and Asia

a shift: a change

to subsidize: to finance, support

a fluctuation: a movement or change

sovereignty: self-government, supremacy

the forefront: in the position of most importance, vanguard

to reinvigorate: to revitalize, bring back to life

momentous: important, eventful

Post-Reading

1. What is the writer's main message in this essay?

   _____

   _____

2. Reread the thesis statement of "The Fall." Is the thesis stated or implied?

   _____

3. **a.** In Paragraph 2, the writer explains that one effect of the Soviet breakup is the new market economy. What examples does the writer give to show that countries are now in a market economy?

   _____

   _____

   b. In Paragraph 4, the author writes about ethnic minorities and their problems. Which minorities are specifically mentioned, and what problems are they having?

   _____

   _____

4. In Paragraph 2, find a word that has approximately the same meaning as the word *shift* and write it

   here. _____

5. Find the boldfaced vocabulary word in the final paragraph of this essay. Write a synonym of that

   word here. _____

Building Better Sentences: For further practice, go to Practice 16 on page 202 in Appendix 1.

Developing a Cause-Effect Essay

In this next section, you will work on cause-effect essays as you make an outline, write supporting information, study connectors, and choose a topic. Practicing these skills will help you write an effective cause-effect essay.

ACTIVITY 3 Outlining Practice

Complete the following two outlines with a partner. The first one outlines the causes of bullying behavior (focus-on-causes method), and the second one outlines the effects of bullying on the young people who are being bullied (focus-on-effects method). Use your imagination, knowledge of the topic, and understanding of essay organization. Be sure to pay attention to the thesis statements and use them to help you complete the outlines.

Focus-on-Causes Outline

Topic: The causes of bullying behavior

I. Introduction (Paragraph 1)

  A. Hook: _____

  _____

  B. Thesis statement: Bullying behavior can occur for many reasons, some of which are _____

  _____

  _____

  _____

II. Body

  A. Paragraph 2 (Cause 1) topic sentence: Teens often begin bullying because they want to control those who are weaker than they are.

SUPPORT

  1. Bullying gives young people an identity—they become well-known in school.

  2. Bullying makes them feel powerful.

  3. _____

  B. Paragraph 3 (Cause 2) topic sentence: _____

  _____

SUPPORT

  1. In many families, both parents work outside the home.

  2. Parents often do not have time to pay attention to their children's needs.

  3. Parents may not be aware that their children are exhibiting aggressive behavior both inside and outside the home.

  C. Paragraph 4 (Cause 3) topic sentence: _____

  _____

SUPPORT

  1. They use violence as a way of identifying themselves.

  2. They may have emotional problems.

  3. Being known for bad behavior is better than not being known at all.

III. Conclusion (Paragraph 5) (restated thesis): _____

  _____

  _____

The best way to stop young people from bullying and abusing their peers is to educate the public—including teachers, parents, and other children—that bullying is an absolutely unacceptable behavior. Only then will there be a decrease in the number of bullying incidents in school.

Focus-on-Effects Outline

Topic: The effects of bullying on the victim

  I. Introduction (Paragraph 1)

    A. Hook: _____

    _____

    B. Thesis statement: When young people bully others, the effects felt by the weaker student can lead to serious, even deadly, consequences.

 II. Body

    A. Paragraph 2 (Effect 1) topic sentence: Students who are bullied tend to withdraw from society.

      1. They often stop communicating with parents and friends.

      2. They want to hide this embarrassing situation, which can lead to lying.

      3. _____

SUPPORT

B. Paragraph 3 (Effect 2) topic sentence: _____

_____

SUPPORT

   1. Students lose self-esteem and start questioning their own personalities, thinking that maybe they deserve this bad treatment.

   2. They may start focusing only on the bully.

   3. Their outlook on life may become darker and darker as the bullying continues.

C. Paragraph 4 (Effect 3) topic sentence: If teens become damaged by the bullying, they may do almost anything to get out of the situation.

SUPPORT

   1. They may try to escape from their painful reality by engaging in dangerous activities.

   2. They might think about a plan of revenge.

   3. _____

III. Conclusion (Paragraph 5) (restated thesis): _____

_____

When young people are victims of bullies, there is a strong chance that they will suffer many negative consequences, not only from the bullies themselves but also as they begin to separate from society. For so many years, bullying was considered a normal part of growing up. However, with the increase of teen anguish due to bullying and the millions of dollars spent on long-term therapy, one has to wonder if bullying should be considered a "normal" activity. In order to ensure a stable and healthy society, individuals need to take a harder look at this negative behavior that hurts not only the bullied child and the bully, but the family and society as a whole.

ACTIVITY 4   **Supporting Information**

The cause-effect essay on the next page is missing the supporting information. As you read the essay, work with a partner to write supporting sentences for each paragraph. If you need more space, use a separate piece of paper. After you finish, compare your supporting information with that of other students.

Television at Its Worst

1   Mr. Stevenson has just come home from a terribly tiring day at work. The first thing he does, after taking off his tie and shoes, is plop down on the couch and turn on the television. Does this sound like a normal routine? It should, because Mr. Stevenson's actions are repeated by millions around the world. People use television to relax and to forget about their daily troubles. However, what started out decades ago as an exciting, new type of family entertainment is currently being blamed for serious problems, especially in children. Many researchers now claim that too much television is not good for kids. They have a point; watching too much TV often does have negative effects on children and adolescents.

2   One negative effect of TV on kids is laziness. _____

_____

_____

_____

_____

_____

3   Another problem with TV watching and kids is that children may have difficulty distinguishing between what is real and what is not. _____

_____

_____

_____

_____

_____

4   Finally, television may lead children to _____

_____

_____

_____

_____

5   Television has changed over the years to include more and more programs that are inappropriate for children. For TV to once again play a more positive role in children's lives, something must be done. Society cannot just continue to wonder why children are behaving poorly. It is time to change TV viewing behavior.

Building Better Sentences: For further practice, go to Practice 17 on page 203 in Appendix 1.

Grammar for Writing

Connectors for Cause-Effect Essays

Connectors show relationships between ideas in sentences and paragraphs. In cause-effect essays, writers commonly use the connecting words and phrases in the following charts.

Connectors That Show Cause

To Introduce Sentences	Examples
As a result of + Noun, Subject + Verb.	**As a result of the rain**, we all got wet.
Because of + Noun, Subject + Verb.	**Because of** the rain, we all got wet.
Due to + Noun, Subject + Verb.	**Due to** the rain, we all got wet.
As Part of an Adverb Clause	**Examples**
Because + Subject + Verb, Subject + Verb.	**Because** it rained, we all got wet.
Since + Subject + Verb, Subject + Verb.	**Since** it rained, we all got wet.

Connectors That Show Effect

Between Sentences	Examples
For this reason, Subject + Verb.	Out of the blue, it started to rain heavily and none of us was prepared for it. **For this reason,** we all got wet.
Therefore, Subject + Verb.	**Therefore,** we all got wet.
As a result, Subject + Verb.	**As a result,** we all got wet.
Thus, Subject + Verb.	**Thus,** we all got wet.
Consequently, Subject + Verb.	**Consequently,** we all got wet.

For a more complete list of connectors, see the *Brief Writer's Handbook with Activities*, pages 180–181.

ACTIVITY 5 Connectors

Read the next essay (focus-on-effects method) and underline the appropriate connector in each set of parentheses. Refer to the charts above, if necessary.

Effects of Studying Abroad

1   Globalization has impacted all aspects of modern-day life, from a country's commerce and politics to a family's everyday decision-making strategy at the grocery store. One of the elements of globalization that is of particular interest in the field of education is study abroad programs. Host countries and institutions are eager to accept international students while the students are intrigued by the possibility of international travel. Studying abroad has become an opportunity that is available to many students, especially those at the university level. Certainly, studying abroad is not for everyone; (however / as a result), for those students who experience it, the positive effects will stay with them forever.

2   One important effect of studying abroad is a student's greater understanding of a different educational system. The curriculum, **availability** and types of lectures, and the educational environment as a whole will differ from that of the student's home country. At first the student may be confused, but this **exposure** to a different curriculum will broaden his or her educational horizons **in the long run**. (For this reason / As a result of) the new academic culture, the student will be able to better appreciate his or her own educational setting later at home.

the availability: accessibility, ease of use

the exposure: experience with, introduction to

in the long run: in time, ultimately

3   Individuals who study abroad also develop their understanding of a different popular culture. Even if the host country's language is the same, there are many cultural experiences that the student will have. From learning how to live with a host family to finding the least expensive grocery store, the student will come across new and sometimes **frustrating** customs and **conventions**. (Since / Consequently), he or she will need to adapt to rules and behaviors that are unfamiliar. The comfortable, well-known lifestyle of the student's past has disappeared and been replaced with the newness of everything. This life exercise may be difficult in the beginning of the study abroad period, but it becomes easier as time passes and the student develops a better understanding of the host country.

frustrating: annoying, difficult, exasperating

a convention: rule

4   Finally, studying abroad gives students the opportunity to serve as ambassadors for their home countries. A foreign student on a university campus can be an uncommon sight. The host institution, including the local **student body**, will form an impression of the student's culture based on interactions with him or her. (As a result / Due to), the student should remember to represent his or her country and culture in the best possible light.

the student body: student population at a particular school

5   To summarize, there are a number of effects of studying abroad, not only for the student but also for the host institution. While some of the experiences may seem difficult at the time, the long-term effects can be considered positive. This is in large part (because of / because) globalization in the education **sector**.

a sector: area, part

Building Better Sentences: For further practice, go to Practice 18 on page 204 in Appendix 1.

Grammar for Writing

Noun Clauses

Noun clauses take the place of a noun or a noun phrase in a sentence. Study the following chart:

Function	Noun **Phrase**	Noun **Clause**
Subject	**The pizza** was delicious.	**What I ate for dinner** was delicious.
Object	I don't know **the answer**.	I don't know **what the answer is**.
Object of preposition	No one is interested in **his remarks**.	No one is interested in **what he said**.
Subject complement	The main problem is **a lack of workers**.	The main problem is **that there are not enough workers**.

Noun clauses begin with the following connectors:

Adverbial Connector	*Wh-* Connectors	*Wh*-ever Connectors
if	how, what, when, where,	whatever, whenever, wherever,
that	which, who, whom,	whichever, whoever, whomever
whether	whose, why	

ACTIVITY 6 Identifying Noun Clauses and Adjective Clauses

The following sentences were taken from this unit. Each sentence contains either a noun clause or an adjective clause. Underline the clause (beginning with a connector) in each sentence and identify it as either a noun clause (NC) or an adjective clause (AC).

_____ 1. A system that took so long to build will probably need as much time, if not more, to truly adapt to the free enterprise system.

_____ 2. Another problem with TV watching and kids is that children may have difficulty distinguishing between reality and fantasy.

_____ 3. Governments that once had subsidized the costs of basic necessities are now letting competition and external factors determine the prices of these items.

_____ 4. In fact, many people who have told the truth to loved ones, only to see the negative reaction, wish they *had* told a white lie.

_____ 5. It is true that everyone makes a blunder from time to time.

_____ 6. Parents may not be aware that their children are exhibiting aggressive behavior both inside and outside the home.

_____ 7. Society cannot just continue to wonder why children are behaving poorly.

_____ 8. These types of stories typically show children that "honesty is the best policy."

_____ 9. What started out decades ago as an exciting type of family entertainment is currently being blamed for problems, especially in children.

_____10. Where their ancestors are from does not matter to them as much as their current homeland.

Choosing Words Carefully

In all writing, including cause-effect essays, attention to precise language is important. Wordiness, or using unnecessary words, is a common problem for many writers. If you can eliminate wordiness from your writing, your essays will be clearer and easier to read.

Wordiness

Some writers think that the more words they use, the better an essay will sound. However, in academic writing in English, it is important to be as concise as possible. Unnecessary words and phrases do not improve your writing. Instead, they make it hard for readers to understand what you want to say.

The list on the left contains common **wordy** phrases. Good writers use the fewest words possible to make a point. In other words, they are being **concise**. Try to avoid using the phrases on the left; substitute them with the phrases on the right.

Wordy	Concise
at that point in time	at that time
despite the fact that + Subject + Verb	despite + Noun
for all intents and purposes	Ø—use nothing
for the purpose of	for
in my opinion, I believe…	in my opinion… *or* I believe…
in the event that	if
in the final analysis	finally
in the vicinity of	near
it goes without saying	Ø—use nothing
it seems unnecessary to point out	Ø—use nothing
made a statement saying	said
the reason why is	because
when all is said and done	Ø—use nothing

ACTIVITY 7 **Wordiness**

The introductory paragraph on the next page is from a cause-effect essay, and it contains seven examples of wordy phrases. Underline them as you find them. Then, on a separate piece of paper, rewrite the paragraph without the wordy phrases and make it more concise. Note: There is more than one correct way of rewriting this paragraph.

Fat-Free Food

In my opinion, I believe that the fat-free food industry is a tremendous money-making business. In fact, recent research has shown that fat-free products are considered only a minor prescription for the purpose of losing weight. Nutritionists have made statements saying that, for all intents and purposes, more important steps to losing weight are exercising and eating well-balanced meals. Despite the fact that this information has appeared, many people still seem to believe that, when all is said and done, eating fat-free food is the best dieting method. The content of the following essay shows some interesting reasons for this fat-free phenomenon.

Redundancy

Redundancy—a kind of wordiness—is the unnecessary repetition of information. When you write, you may want to impress your readers with an eloquent essay that is full of thought-provoking information. One way that writers often try to do this is by loading up on information. You may think, "The more information I have in my essay, the more my readers will enjoy it." This is not usually the case, especially if, instead of adding information, you repeat what you have already said. Repetition can occur in the wording of short phrases as well as in sentences.

Redundant phrases. The list on the left contains commonly used redundant phrases. Try to avoid them in your writing. (If you are not sure why the phrases are redundant, look up the meanings of the two words.)

Change	To
collaborate together	collaborate
completely unanimous	unanimous
courthouse building	courthouse
descend downward	descend
erupt violently	erupt
exactly identical	identical
free gift	gift
loud explosion	explosion
merge together	merge
repeat again	repeat
unexpected surprise	surprise

Look at the example sentences below. The first sentence contains the same information as the second sentence.

Redundant Sentence   The United States is the most influential power in the world. Partly because of its abundant material resources and stable political system, this country has great influence in global affairs.

Concise Sentence   The United States has a great influence in global affairs in part because of its abundant material resources and stable political system.

Underline the redundant information in this paragraph. Then compare your work with a partner's.

Extrasensory Perception

Many people love to watch science-fiction stories on TV or at the movies. TV shows and films, such as *Star Trek*, are popular not only because they creatively show how future life might be in 300 years, but also because they introduce us to characters from other worlds, planets, and galaxies. Perhaps one of the most popular kinds of characters in these futuristic programs is a person with ESP, or extrasensory perception. ESP is a sense that allows one person to read the mind of another without the exchange of words. These characters, who can read minds and know the innermost thoughts and secrets of other people, often use their gift in less than noble ways. One must remember, however, that these scenes take place in an untrue and fictitious situation. A more interesting concept is to think about what would really happen if ordinary, everyday people possessed ESP.

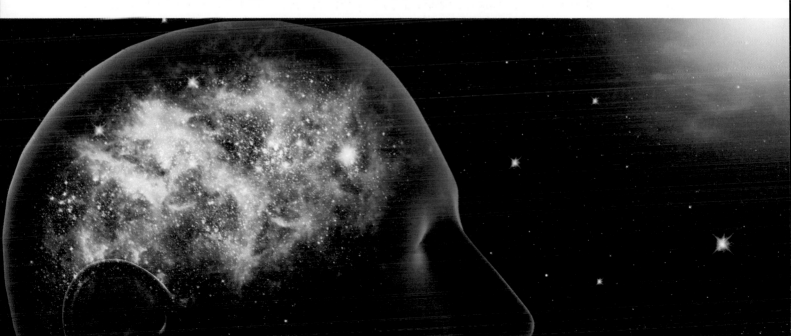

Building Better Vocabulary

Word Associations

Circle the word or phrase that is most closely related to the word or phrase on the left. If necessary, use a dictionary to check the meaning of words you do not know.

	A	**B**
1. shift*	moving	unmoving
2. an ideology*	beliefs	smart
3. momentous	for a short time	important
4. fluctuation*	stable	unstable
5. abroad	inside the country	overseas
6. to rejoice	happy feelings	sad feelings
7. the forefront	new ideas	old ideas
8. availability*	presence	thought
9. exposure*	hidden	open
10. a blunder	a mistake	an opinion

*Indicates words that are part of the Academic Word List. See pages 183–184 for a complete list.

ACTIVITY 10 **Using Collocations**

Fill in each blank with the word or phrase on the left that most naturally completes the phrase on the right. If necessary, use a dictionary to check the meaning of words you do not know.

1. lunch / time	to have a difficult _____
2. on / to	one negative effect of TV _____ people
3. out of / up to	to get _____ a bad situation
4. by / for	convenient _____ everyone
5. run / time	in the long _____
6. play / run	to _____ a role
7. in / of	effects _____ studying abroad
8. part / step	a normal _____ of life
9. for / to	to resort _____ an alternative plan
10. in / to	children tend _____ be active

Developing Ideas for Writing

Many writers can think of good topics, but they have trouble developing their topics into essays. One brainstorming method that helps is to ask questions about the topic—*Who? What? Where? When? Why? How?* This process often leads to new ideas that can be used in an essay. Especially for a cause-effect essay, good writers ask the question *Why?*

ACTIVITY 11 **Starting with Questions**

The following questions can all be developed into cause-effect essays. Try to give at least three answers to each question.

1. Why do people gain too much weight?

   _____

   _____

   _____

2. What usually happens after a natural disaster?

   _____

   _____

   _____

3. Why do people quit their jobs?

   _____

   _____

   _____

4. What would happen if the world's biggest economies failed?

   _____

   _____

   _____

5. Why are more and more people studying a second (or third) language?

   _____

   _____

   _____

6. What are the effects of playing a team sport?

   _____

   _____

   _____

7. What are the causes of _____? (Think of your own topic.)

_____

_____

_____

8. What are the effects of _____? (Think of your own topic.)

_____

_____

_____

Brainstorming

In the next activity, you will use a brainstorming technique called **clustering**. Here is an example of clustering; the topic is the effects of ozone depletion on the environment.

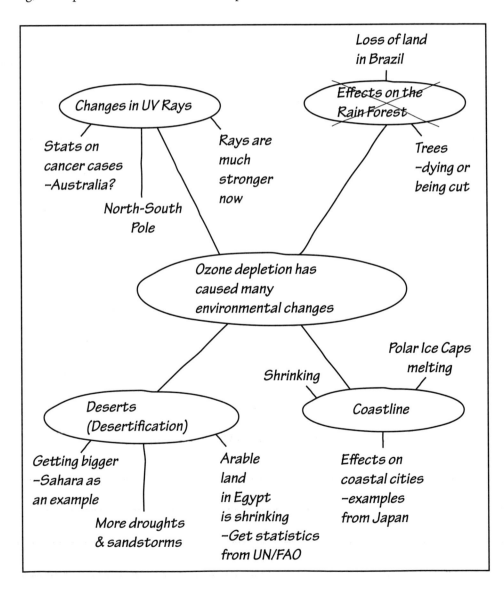

Original Student Writing: Cause-Effect Essay

ACTIVITY 12 Clustering Ideas

Choose a topic from Activity 11. Brainstorm some ideas about your topic using the clustering method. Write all your ideas. When you have finished, cross out the ideas that you do not like or do not want to include in your essay. Explain your brainstorming cluster to a classmate.

ACTIVITY 13 Planning with an Outline

Complete the outline below as a guide to help you brainstorm a more detailed plan for your cause-effect essay. Use your ideas from Activity 12. You may need to use either more or fewer points under each heading. Write in complete sentences where possible.

Topic: _____

  I. Introduction (Paragraph 1)

    A. Hook: _____

    B. Connecting information: _____

    _____

    C. Thesis statement: _____

    _____

 II. Body

    A. Paragraph 2 (first cause or effect) topic sentence: _____

    _____

SUPPORT

      1. _____

      2. _____

      3. _____

    B. Paragraph 3 (second cause or effect) topic sentence: _____

    _____

SUPPORT

      1. _____

      2. _____

      3. _____

C. Paragraph 4 (third cause or effect) topic sentence: _____

_____

SUPPORT

1. _____

2. _____

3. _____

III. Conclusion (paragraph 5)

    A. Restated thesis: _____

_____

    B. Suggestion, opinion, or prediction: _____

_____

Writer's Note

Personal Writing Style

Some writers work well from a detailed outline, and some can write well from a general outline. Some writers write the introduction first, and some write it last. Writing is an individual activity. Use the guidelines in this book and follow the process that works best for you.

ACTIVITY 14 **Peer Editing Your Outline**

Exchange books with a partner and look at Activity 13. Read your partner's outline. Then use Peer Editing Sheet 5 on NGL.Cengage.com/GW4 to help you comment on your partner's outline. Use your partner's feedback to revise your outline. Make sure you have enough information to develop your supporting sentences.

ACTIVITY 15 **Writing a Cause-Effect Essay**

Write a cause-effect essay based on your revised outline from Activity 14. Use at least two of the vocabulary words or phrases presented in Activities 9 and 10. Underline these words and phrases in your essay. Be sure to refer to the seven steps in the writing process in the *Brief Writer's Handbook with Activities* on pages 156–163.

If you need ideas for words and phrases, see the Useful Vocabulary for Better Writing on pages 185–188.

ACTIVITY 16 **Peer Editing Your Essay**

Exchange papers from Activity 15 with a partner. Read your partner's essay. Then use Peer Editing Sheet 6 on NGL.Cengage.com/GW4 to help you comment on your partner's writing. Be sure to offer positive suggestions and comments that will help your partner improve his or her essay. Consider your partner's comments as you revise your own essay.

Additional Topics for Writing

Here are more ideas for topics for a cause-effect essay. Before you write, be sure to refer to the seven steps in the writing process in the *Brief Writer's Handbook with Activities*, on pages 156–163.

PHOTO
TOPIC: Look at the photograph on pages 88–89. As climates change, many parts of the world are experiencing extreme weather such as heavy rains or snow, intense heat without any rain, and powerful storms. What are some effects of extreme weather?

TOPIC 2: Going to college is a dream for many people. Some do the work, graduate, and find good jobs. Other students, however, never finish their university studies. Write an essay about what causes students to drop out of college.

TOPIC 3: Friendships are an integral part of a person's life. Unfortunately, some of these relationships do not last. Write an essay highlighting some of the reasons that friendships sometimes die.

TOPIC 4: Many people enjoy traveling and experiencing other cultures. What are some of the beneficial effects of international travel on an individual?

TOPIC 5: Children are learning to use computers at a very early age. What are some effects (positive or negative) that computers can have on the intellectual development of children?

Timed Writing

How quickly can you write in English? There are many times when you must write quickly such as on a test. It is important to feel comfortable during those times. Timed-writing practice can make you feel better about writing quickly in English.

1. Take out a piece of paper.

2. Read the essay guidelines and the writing prompt.

3. Write a basic outline, including the thesis and your three main points.

4. Write a five-paragraph essay.

5. You have 40 minutes to write your essay.

Cause-Effect Essay Guidelines

- Use the focus-on-causes method.

- Remember to give your essay a title.

- Double-space your essay.

- Write as legibly as possible (if you are not using a computer).

- Select an appropriate principle of organization for your topic.

- Include a short introduction (with a thesis statement), three body paragraphs, and a conclusion.

- Try to give yourself a few minutes before the end of the activity to review your work. Check for spelling, verb tense, and subject-verb agreement mistakes.

Why do people keep pets?

Argument Essays

An endangered Northern spotted owl, a source of much controversy in logging communities of the Pacific Northwest, rests in a fresh clear-cut near Merlin, Oregon.

OBJECTIVES To learn how to write an argument essay
To control tone with modals
To learn to use the *if* clause

Can you persuade someone to agree with your opinion on nature conservation versus industry growth?

What Is an Argument Essay?

In an **argument essay**, the writer's purpose is to persuade the audience to agree with his or her opinion about a controversial topic. In a sociology class, for example, you might write an essay arguing that female military personnel can be as effective as male military personnel in combat missions. In a history class, your essay might try to convince readers that World War I could have been avoided if certain steps had been taken. In an argument essay, sometimes referred to as a **persuasive essay**, the writer states the claim (opinion), gives reasons to support it, and tries to convince the audience that he or she is correct.

Arguing Pro or Con

Choosing a topic that is appropriate for an argument essay is especially important because some things cannot be argued. For example, you cannot argue that a tulip is more beautiful than a daisy because this is an opinion that cannot be supported by facts. However, you can argue that tulips are more popular than daisies and support the argument with facts about florists' sales of the two kinds of flowers.

Here are a few effective topics and thesis statements for an argument essay:

- Marriage before the age of eighteen: People under the age of eighteen should not be allowed to marry.

- Standardized testing: Standardized testing should not be required as part of the application process for a university.

- Fast-food restaurants: Fast-food restaurants ought to list the calorie counts for all the food that they sell.

You can argue either for **(pro)** or against **(con)** these statements. If your topic does not have two viewpoints, your essay will not be effective. Look at the following example of an ineffective topic and thesis statement.

Jazz music: Jazz music began with African Americans.

You cannot argue against this statement because it is a fact. Therefore, you cannot write an argument essay using this thesis statement.

Convincing the Reader

Your job as the writer of an argument essay is to convince your readers that your opinion about a topic (your thesis statement) is the most valid viewpoint. To do this, your essay needs to be balanced—it must include an opposing viewpoint, or **counterargument**. Even though you are arguing one side of an issue (either for or against), you must think about what someone on the other side of the issue would argue. As soon as you give your opponent's point of view, you must offer a **refutation** of it. This means that you refute the other point of view, or show how it is wrong. If you give only your opinion, your essay will sound like propaganda, and your readers will not be convinced of your viewpoint.

ACTIVITY 1 Studying an Argument Essay

This essay argues the use of school uniforms. Discuss the Preview Questions with a classmate. Then read the example essay and answer the questions that follow.

Preview Questions

1. Did you wear a uniform when you went to school? NO

2. Some people believe that children are too materialistic these days. For example, they may be too interested in wearing brand name clothes and shoes. What is your opinion?

The School Uniform Question

1   Individualism is a **fundamental** part of society in many countries. Most people believe in the right to express their own opinion without fear of punishment. This value, however, is coming under fire in an unlikely place—the **public school** classroom. The issue is school uniforms. Should public school students be allowed to make individual decisions about clothing, or should all students be required to wear a uniform? School uniforms are the better choice for three reasons.

2   First, wearing school uniforms would help make students' lives simpler. They would no longer have to decide what to wear every morning, sometimes trying on outfit after outfit in an effort to choose. Uniforms would not only save time but also would eliminate the stress often associated with this chore.

3   Second, school uniforms influence students to act responsibly in groups and as individuals. Uniforms give students the message that school is a special place for learning. In addition, uniforms create a feeling of unity among students. For example, when students do something as a group, such as attend meetings in the auditorium or eat lunch in the cafeteria, the fact that they all wear the same uniform gives them a sense of community. Even more important, statistics show the positive effects that school uniforms have on violence and **truancy**. According to a recent survey in a large school district in Florida, incidents of school violence dropped by 50 percent, attendance and test scores improved, and student suspensions declined approximately 30 percent after school uniforms were introduced.

4   Finally, school uniforms would help make all the students feel equal. Students' standards of living differ greatly from family to family, and some people are **well-off** while others are not. People sometimes forget that school is a place to get an education, not to promote a "fashion show." **Implementing** mandatory school uniforms would make all the students look the same regardless of their financial status. School uniforms would promote pride and help to raise the self-esteem of students who cannot afford to wear expensive clothing.

5   Opponents of mandatory uniforms say that students who wear school uniforms cannot express their individuality. This point has some merit on the surface. However, as stated previously, school is a place to learn, not to **flaunt** wealth and fashion. Society must decide if individual expression through clothing is more valuable than improved educational performance. It is important to remember that school uniforms would be worn only during school hours. Students can express their individuality in the way that they dress outside of the classroom.

6   In conclusion, there are many well-documented benefits of implementing mandatory school uniforms for students. Studies show that students learn better and act more responsibly when they wear uniforms. Public schools should require uniforms in order to benefit both the students and society as a whole.

fundamental: essential, basic

a public school: a school run by the state government and paid for by taxes

truancy: absence without permission

well-off: wealthy

to implement: to put into effect

to flaunt: to show off, display

Post-Reading

1. The topic of this essay is school uniforms. What is the hook in the first paragraph?

_____

_____

2. What is the thesis statement? School uniforms are the better choice for three reasons.

_____

3. Paragraphs 2, 3, and 4 each give a reason for requiring school uniforms. These reasons can be found in the topic sentence of each paragraph. What are the reasons?

   Paragraph 2: Wearing school uniforms would help make students' lives simpler

   Paragraph 3: School uniforms influence students to act responsibly in group and as individuals.

   Paragraph 4: make all the students feel equal.

   _____

4. In Paragraph 4, what supporting information does the writer give to show that uniforms make students equal?

   _____

   _____

   _____

5. Which paragraph presents a counterargument—an argument that is contrary to, or the opposite of, the writer's opinion? _____5_____ What is the counterargument?

   students who wear school uniforms cannot express their individulity.

   _____

6. The writer gives a refutation of the counterargument by showing that it is invalid. What is the writer's refutation?

   5 - School is place to learn.

   _____

   _____

7. Write the sentence from the concluding paragraph that restates the thesis.

_____

_____

_____

8. Reread the concluding paragraph. What is the writer's opinion about this issue?

_____

_____

_____

Building Better Sentences: For further practice, go to Practice 19 on page 205 in Appendix 1.

Developing an Argument Essay

Outlining

ACTIVITY 2 Outlining Practice

The following outline, which is designed for an argument essay, is missing some supporting information. Work with a partner to complete the outline. Use your imagination, knowledge of the topic, and understanding of essay organization to complete this outline with your partner. After you finish, compare your supporting information with other students' work.

Topic: Mandatory physical education in school علاقه بسیار سال و سوال

I. Introduction (Paragraph 1)

Thesis statement: Physical education classes should be required for all public school students in all grades.

II. Body

A. Paragraph 2 (Pro argument 1) topic sentence: Physical education courses promote children's general health.

SUPPORT

1. Researchers have proved that exercise has maximum benefit if done regularly.

2. Students can get used to daily exercise and make it a good habit.

3. Students should learn the importance of physical fitness at an early age.

B. Paragraph 3 (Pro argument 2) topic sentence: Physical education teaches children transferable life skills.

SUPPORT

1. Kids learn about teamwork while playing team sports.

2. Kids learn about the benefits of healthy competition.

3. Kids learn about how to draw.

C. Paragraph 4 (Pro argument 3) topic sentence: School have the resources to make sure children are exercising properly.

SUPPORT

1. Trained physical education teachers can teach more effectively than parents.

2. Physical education teachers can usually point students toward new and interesting sports.

3. Schools generally have the appropriate facilities and equipment.

D. Paragraph 5 (counterargument and refutation)

SUPPORT

1. Counterargument: Some parents might disagree and claim that only academic subjects should be taught in school.

2. Refutation: Then again, most parents do not have the time or the resources to see to it that their children are getting enough exercise.

III. Conclusion (Paragraph 6) (restated thesis): Schools are the perfect place to get all children involved in sporting activites. for students

Physical education has often been downplayed as a minor part of daily school life. If its benefits are taken into account and if schools adopt a 12-year fitness plan, the positive results will foster a new awareness of not only physical fitness but also communication skills.

Adding Supporting Information

ACTIVITY 3 **Studying the Supporting Information in an Example Essay**

In this essay, the writer argues about celebrity lifestyles and privacy. Discuss the Preview Questions with a classmate. Then read and study the example essay, and fill in the missing supporting information in the spaces provided.

Preview Questions

1. Would you like to live the life of a celebrity? What are some of the advantages of being a "star"?

2. List a few famous people who have had difficulty dealing with their celebrity status and lifestyles. Why do you think they had these problems?

Essay 20

Privacy for Celebrities

1   The year 1997 will always be remembered as the year of celebrity tragedy. It was the year when Diana, Princess of Wales was killed in a horrific car accident. For weeks, reporters discussed who was at fault. Yes, her chauffeur was driving at an extremely high speed, but the car was being chased by the **paparazzi**. Many people decided that Princess Diana was a victim of these overly aggressive photographers. Was she? Or was it understood that celebrity status came with the compromise of little or no privacy? The debate on celebrity privacy continues, and it seems that almost everyone has an opinion. For many, the concept is simple: privacy ends when celebrity status is achieved. The stars know this, and they need to stop complaining about it.

the paparazzi:
celebrity photographers

2   Being followed and **harassed** should not be a surprise as it is an expected part of being a celebrity.

جلدیر

کر گوار

و انا رو

قوقی

to be harassed: to be bothered by someone

_____

_____

_____

_____

3   The media is basically in charge of a person's celebrity status; no media attention equals no stardom.

_____

_____

_____

_____

4   Celebrities are often role models, so they need to be prepared for the paparazzi's cameras at all times.

_____

_____

_____

_____

5   Some people say that even the most famous people need their privacy, especially in tragic situations. However, celebrity status does not come with the option of choosing the best time to be photographed or followed. Stars knew about the effects of stardom, such as lack of privacy, before they became famous, so they must take the good with the bad.

_____

_____

_____

_____

6   Once an actor, singer, or athlete becomes famous, the notion of being a **reluctant** star does not make sense. In essence, celebrities **give up** their privacy the minute they achieve stardom. As responsible members of society, they need to embrace this part of their celebrity status in the same way that they embrace fame, fortune, and **adoration** from their fans.

reluctant: unwilling

to give up: to surrender, agree not to own

the adoration: high regard, worship

Building Better Sentences: For further practice, go to Practice 20 on page 205 in Appendix 1.

Choosing a Topic

طاب و جب کس سب ندار
و ق جاول

Writing Pro and Con Thesis Statements

Read the following list of topics for argument essays. For each topic, write a pro (for) thesis statement and a con (against) thesis statement related to the topic. Then compare your statements with your classmates' statements. The first one has been done for you.

1. **Topic: Women in the military**

   Pro thesis statement: _In a society where women are chief executive officers of companies, leaders of nations, and family breadwinners, there is no reason why they should not play an active role in the military._

   Con thesis statement: _Women should not be allowed to fight in the military because they do not have the strength or endurance required in combat._

2. **Topic: Using animals in disease research**

   Pro thesis statement: _____

   _____

   Con thesis statement: _____

   _____

3. **Topic: Driver's license age restrictions**

   Pro thesis statement: _There must be a restriction on the age at which the driver obtains the licence for security reasons._

   Con thesis statement: _The driver's licence is supposed to be given to anyone who can drive regardless of age._

4. Topic: Space exploration

   Pro thesis statement: _____

   _____

   Con thesis statement: _____

   _____

5. Topic: Internet privacy

   Pro thesis statement: _____

   _____

   Con thesis statement: _____

   _____

Grammar for Writing

Controlling Tone with Modals

In argument essays, good writers are aware of how their arguments sound. Are they too strong? Not strong enough? Certain words can help control the tone of your argument.

Modals can change the tone of a sentence. Modals such as *must* and *had/better* make a verb stronger. Other modals such as *may, might, should, can,* and *could* make a verb softer. Remember to use modals to strengthen or soften your verbs.

Asserting a Point

Strong modals such as *must* and *had better* help writers to assert their main points. When you use these words, readers know where you stand on an issue.

Examples:

The facts clearly show that researchers **must** stop unethical animal testing.

People who value their health **had better** stop smoking now.

Acknowledging an Opposing Point

Weaker modals such as *may, might, could, can,* and *would* help writers make an opposing opinion sound weak. You acknowledge an opposing point when you use *may,* for example, but this weak modal shows that the statement is not strong and can be refuted more easily. In short, the use of *may* and *might* is crucial to constructing a proper refutation and then counterargument.

Here is an example from the essay in Activity 2 (page 119):

Some parents (might) disagree and claim that only academic subjects should be taught in school. Then again, most parents do not have the time or the resources to see to it that their children are getting enough exercise.

Other Examples:

While it (may) be true that people have eaten meat for a long time, the number one killer of Americans now is heart disease, caused in part by the consumption of large amounts of animal fat.

Some citizens (may) be against mandatory military service, but those who do serve in the military often have a strong sense of pride and personal satisfaction.

Read the following argument essay. Circle the modal in parentheses that you feel is more appropriate.

Essay 21

Issues in Morality

1   In order to become a member of the European Union (EU), a country (must) prove that it handles human rights in a humane and civil way. One major concern of the EU is the death penalty. In fact, the death penalty is not allowed in any of the EU countries. To that end, those countries that want membership must prove that their laws protect the human lives of even the cruelest of criminals. This point of view, however, is not shared by all. Countries such as Singapore, Japan, South Korea, and the United States allow for the death penalty. In fact, the death penalty (should) be allowed in all countries.

2   The first reason for allowing the death penalty is for the **sake** of punishment itself. Most people agree that criminals who commit serious crimes (**1.** might / (should)) be separated from society. The punishment (**2.** will / (ought to)) depend on the degree of the crime.

sake: benefit, well being

The death penalty, the most severe form of punishment, ends criminals' lives. It seems reasonable that this **severe** punishment be reserved for those who commit the most serious of crimes.

3   The second reason to allow for the death penalty is financial. The government (**3.** should / will) not have to spend a lot of money on criminals. Next to a death sentence, the most severe punishment is a life sentence in prison, where the government (**4.** might / has to) take care of criminals until they die naturally. These criminals do not actively improve society, but society must provide them free housing and food. It is unfair to use a country's taxes for such a purpose.

4   Finally, one must look at the government and its **role** in society. Society agrees that government has **legitimate** power to make, judge, and carry out the laws; as a result, it (**5.** may / should) also have the power to decide if criminals should die. The death penalty is like any other sentence. If one believes that the government has the right to charge a fine or put criminals into jail, then the government (**6.** could / must) also have the same power to decide the fate of a prisoner's life.

5   The opponents of the death penalty (**7.** must / might) say that nobody has the right to decide who should die, including the government. However, when the government sends soldiers into war, in some way, it is deciding those soldiers' fate; some will live, and some will be killed. As long as the government makes decisions to send its citizens to the battlefield, it has a right to put criminals to death.

6   There are many good reasons to allow for the death penalty. Certainly not every criminal (**8.** can / should) be put to death. Still, capital punishment (**9.** ought to / will) be viewed as the harshest form of punishment. If no alternate punishment (**10.** can / should) reform a murderer, then capital punishment is the best thing that can be done for that person and for society. Europe has gotten it wrong.

severe: harsh, strict

role: position, function

legitimate: legal, lawful

Building Better Sentences: For further practice, go to Practice 21 on page 206 in Appendix 1.

Counterargument and Refutation

The key technique to persuading the reader that your viewpoint is valid is to support it in every paragraph. While this is not a problem in the first few paragraphs of your essay the **counterargument** goes against your thesis statement. Consequently, every counterargument that you include in your essay needs a refutation. A **refutation** is a response to the counterargument that disproves it.

For example, imagine that you are having an argument with a friend about your topic. She disagrees with your opinion. What do you think will be her strongest argument against your point of view? How will you respond to this counterargument? Your answer is your refutation.

Look at the following excerpts from two argument essays in this unit. The counterarguments are in *italics* and the refutations are underlined.

From Essay 19:

Opponents of mandatory uniforms say that students who wear school uniforms cannot express their individuality. This point has some merit on the surface. However, as stated previously school is a place to learn, not to flaunt wealth and fashion.

From Essay 20:

Some people say that even the most famous people need their privacy, especially in tragic situations. However, celebrity status does not come with the option of choosing the best time to be photographed or followed. Stars knew about the effects of stardom, for example, lack of privacy, before they became famous, so they must take the good with the bad.

As you can see, what begins as a counterargument ends up as another reason in support of your opinion.

ACTIVITY 6 **Writing a Refutation**

Read each counterargument. Then write a one-line refutation. Remember to use a contrasting connection word to begin your refutation.

1. Parents of extremely young beauty pageant contestants believe that these competitive contests help build their children's confidence.

   _____

   _____

   _____

   _____

2. A majority of health insurance companies do not provide financial coverage for preventive wellness activities like nutrition management classes or gym memberships, stating that they are too costly to manage.

   _____

   _____

   _____

   _____

3. Opponents of the fast-food ban in high schools insist that students should have the freedom to eat whatever they wish.

_____

_____

_____

_____

Avoiding Faulty Logic

Good writers want to convince readers to agree with their arguments—their reasons and conclusions. If your arguments are not logical, you will not persuade your readers. Logic can help prove your point and disprove your opponent's point—and perhaps change your reader's mind about an issue. If you use faulty logic (logic not based on fact), readers will not believe you or take your position seriously.

This section presents a few logical errors that writers sometimes make in argument essays. Try to avoid these errors in your writing.

Events Related Only by Sequence

When one event happens, it does not necessarily cause a second event to happen, even if one follows the other in time.

Example: Henry went to the football game, and then he had a car accident. Therefore, football games cause car accidents.

Problem: The two events may have happened in that order, but do not mislead the reader into thinking that the first action was responsible for the second.

Appeal to Authority

Using famous names may often help you prove or disprove your point. However, be sure to use the name logically and in the proper context.

Example: Beyoncé is a good singer. As a result, she would make a good judge of orchestra conductors.

Problem: While Beyoncé may be a good singer, this quality will not necessarily make her a good judge of orchestra conductors.

Sweeping Generalizations

Words such as _all_, _always_, and _never_ are too broad and cannot be supported.

Example: Everyone is interested in improving the quality of education.

Problem: Really? Everyone? What about a 90-year-old woman who does not have enough money to pay for her medicine? Her immediate concerns are probably not on improving education. She wants her medicine.

Hasty Generalizations (Insufficient Statistics)

Hasty generalizations are just what they sound like—making quick judgments based on inadequate or not enough information. This kind of logical fallacy is a common error in argument writing.

Example: A woman is driving through a small town. She passes three cars, all of which are white pickup trucks. She then writes in her report describing the town that everyone in this town drives a white pickup truck.

Problem: The woman only saw three vehicles. The town actually has over 100 cars. The number of cars that she saw was too small for her to come to that conclusion.

Loaded Words

Some words contain positive or negative connotations. Try to avoid them when you make an argument. Your readers may think you are trying to appeal to them by using these emotionally packed words. In fact, you want to persuade the reader by using logical arguments, not emotional rants.

Example: The blue-flag freedom fighters won the war against the green-flag guerrillas.

Problem: The terms *freedom fighters* (positive) and *guerrillas* (negative) may influence the readers' opinion about the two groups without any support for the bias.

Either/Or Arguments

When you argue a point, be careful not to limit the outcome choices to only two or three. In fact, there are often a multitude of choices. When you offer only two scenarios, you are essentially trying to frighten the reader into your beliefs.

Example: The instructor must either return the tests or dismiss the class.

Problem: This statement implies that only two choices are available to the instructor.

ACTIVITY 7 Faulty Logic

Read the following paragraph, and underline all the uses of faulty logic. Write the kind of error each one is above the words.

Paragraph 3

Penny Wise

Next week, our fine upstanding citizens will go to the polls to vote for or against a penny sales tax for construction of a new stadium. This law, if passed, will cause extreme hardship for local residents. Our taxes are high enough as it is, so why do our city's apathetic leaders think that we will run happily to the polls and vote "yes"? If we take a look at what happened to our sister city as a result of a similar bill, we will see that this new tax will have negative effects. Last year, that city raised its sales tax by one percent. Only three weeks later, the city was nearly destroyed by a riot in the streets. If we want to keep our fair city as it is, we must either vote "no" on the ballot question or live in fear of violence.

Grammar for Writing

Using the *if* Clause

In Unit 3, you reviewed adverb clauses. In this section, you will work on one specific type of adverb clause, the *if* clause. *If* clauses explain a condition that is necessary for a specific outcome. Study the following examples:

Time	*If* Clause / Situation	Outcome
General	If it **is** too hot,	we **turn on** the air conditioning.
Future	If it **is** too hot,	we **will turn on** the air conditioning.
		we **can turn on** the air conditioning.
		we **may turn on** the air conditioning.
		we **might turn on** the air conditioning.
Present	If the restaurant **opened** at noon, (The restaurant does not open at noon.)	we **could eat** lunch there.
		we **would eat** lunch there.
		we **might eat** lunch there.
Past	If the students **had asked** questions during the lecture, (They did not ask questions during the lecture.)	they **would have understood** the concepts better.
		they **might have understood** the concepts better.
		they **could have understood** the concepts better.

ACTIVITY 8 **Identifying and Labeling *if* Clauses**

The following sentences were taken from this unit. Each sentence contains an *if* clause. Underline the verbs in both parts of the sentence. In the space provided, identify the *if* clause as either past (P), present (PR), or future (F) conditional.

_____ 1. If we believe that the government has the right to put criminals into jail, then the government should also have the same power to decide the fate of a prisoner's life.

_____ 2. If no punishment can reform a murderer, then the death penalty is the best thing that can be done for that person and for society.

_____ 3. If we want to keep our fair city as it is, we must either vote "no" on the ballot question or live in fear of violence.

_____ 4. If schools adopt a 12-year fitness plan, the positive results will foster a new awareness of not only physical fitness but also communication skills.

_____ 5. Researchers have proved that exercise has maximum benefit if it is done regularly.

_____ 6. World War I could have been avoided if certain steps had been taken.

_____ 7. If this law is passed, it will cause extreme hardship for local residents.

Citing Sources to Avoid Plagiarism

When writing argument essays, it is often helpful to find facts, figures, or quotes to help support your ideas. With the ease of the Internet, however, we may forget to give credit to the person (or article or website) that the information came from. **Plagiarism**—whether done intentionally or unintentionally—is the act of taking others' words without properly giving credit to the source. Plagiarism is considered a very serious offense in academia and should be avoided at all costs. The penalty for plagiarism can be very severe.

After you have decided that the information you have found in a source is appropriate to support your ideas, you need to insert it in your essay correctly. There are two choices:

1. **Quoting.**   If the information is not too long, you can put it in quotation marks. It is a good idea to introduce the quote with a phrase, such as *According to (name of source), "(exact words used by that source)."* By using this strategy, you not only acknowledge the source but also show that the information is taken word for word. Be careful, however, not to use too many quotations in any particular paragraph. Remember, the reader is looking for *your* voice, not someone else's.

    Example of quoting:

    According to http://www.webhealth.org, "Children need between three and six servings of vegetables daily to maintain a healthy diet."

2. **Paraphrasing.**   Another method of avoiding plagiarism is to paraphrase your source's information. That is, you put the information in your own words. You still need to explain where the information came from even if you changed the words, but you do not need to use quotation marks.

    Example of paraphrasing:

    According to http://www.webhealth.org, in order for a diet to be considered healthy kids should eat a fair number of vegetables every day.

Your instructor can help you if you are unsure of when, where, or exactly how to cite information. In addition, librarians and other school support services often have extensive information on methods of avoiding plagiarism. The key to using outside sources correctly is to be diligent in citing the source you use and to ask questions if you are unsure of how to complete this task. For more information on citing sources, see the *Brief Writer's Handbook with Activities*, pages 181–182.

Building Better Vocabulary

ACTIVITY 9   Word Associations

Circle the word or phrase that is most closely related to the word or phrase on the left. If necessary, use a dictionary to check the meaning of words you do not know.

	A	B
1. fundamental*	important	not important
2. truancy	students	teachers
3. to implement*	to put into effect	to stop using

4. paparazzi	chef	photographer
5. harassed	bothered	calm
6. reluctant*	to not want to do something	to want to do something
7. give up	start	stop
8. adoration	boredom	love
9. an excerpt	a portion	a topic
10. to take into account	to consider	to recommend

*Indicates words that are part of the Academic Word List. See pages 183–184 for a complete list.

ACTIVITY 10 **Using Collocations**

Fill in each blank with the word on the left that most naturally completes the phrase on the right. If necessary, use a dictionary to check the meaning of words you do not know.

1. fire / screams   to come under _____

2. through / with   to be associated _____

3. dictionaries / community   a sense of _____

4. apartment / expression   individual _____

5. complain / complaining   need to stop _____

6. make / take   to _____ the good with the bad

7. do / make   to _____ some changes

8. seconds / times   to be ready at all _____

9. living / working   standard of _____

10. by / of   in fear _____

Original Student Writing: Argument Essay

Brainstorming

Brainstorming will help you get started with your argument essay. In this section, you will choose any method of brainstorming that works for you and develop supporting information.

ACTIVITY 11 **Choosing a Topic**

Follow the steps below to develop ideas for an argument essay.

1. First, choose a thesis statement from the statements that you wrote in Activity 4 on pages 122–123 or choose any other topic and thesis statement that you want to write about. Remember that the topic must have more than one point of view to qualify as an argument.

   Essay topic: _____

   Thesis statement: _____

   _____

2. Now brainstorm ideas about your topic. Write everything you can think of that supports your argument. You may want to begin by answering this question about your thesis statement: *Why do I believe this?*

3. Look at your brainstorming information again. Choose three or four reasons that support your thesis most effectively and circle them. You now know what your major supporting information will be.

4. Now that you have written your thesis statement and a few reasons to support it, it is time to give attention to opposing points of view. On the lines below, write one counterargument and a refutation for your argument essay.

   Counterargument: _____

   _____

   _____

   Refutation: _____

   _____

   _____

5. Remember to include a restatement of your thesis and your opinion about the issue in your conclusion.

If you need ideas for words and phrases, see the Useful Vocabulary for Better Writing on pages 185–188.

Complete the following outline as a guide to help you brainstorm a more detailed plan for your argument essay. Use your ideas from Activity 11. You may need to use either more or fewer points under each heading. Write complete sentences where possible.

Topic: _____

  1. Introduction (Paragraph 1)

   A. Hook: _____

   B. Connecting information: _____

   _____

   C. Thesis statement: _____

   _____

  2. Body

   A. Paragraph 2 (first reason) topic sentence: _____

   _____

   SUPPORT
   1. _____
   2. _____
   3. _____

   B. Paragraph 3 (second reason) topic sentence: _____

   _____

   SUPPORT
   1. _____
   2. _____
   3. _____

   C. Paragraph 4 (third reason) topic sentence: _____

   _____

   SUPPORT
   1. _____
   2. _____
   3. _____

D. Paragraph 5 (counterargument and refutation)

   1. Counterargument: _____

   _____

   2. Refutation: _____

   _____

3. Conclusion (Paragraph 6)

   A. Restated thesis:

   _____

   _____

   B. Opinion:

   _____

   _____

ACTIVITY 13 Peer Editing Your Outline

Exchange books with a partner and look at Activity 12. Read your partner's outline. Then use Peer Editing Sheet 7 on NGL.Cengage.com/GW4 to help you comment on your partner's outline. Be sure to offer positive suggestions and comments that will help your partner improve his or her writing. Consider your partner's comments as you revise your outline. Make sure you have enough information to develop your supporting sentences.

ACTIVITY 14 Writing an Argument Essay

Write an argument essay based on your revised outline from Activity 12. Use at least two of the vocabulary words or phrases presented in Activities 8 and 9. Underline these words and phrases in your essay. Be sure to refer to the seven steps in the writing process in the *Brief Writer's Handbook with Activities* on pages 156–163.

ACTIVITY 15 Peer Editing Your Essay

Exchange papers from Activity 14 with a partner. Read your partner's essay. Then use Peer Editing Sheet 8 on NGL.Cengage.com/GW4 to help you comment on your partner's writing. Be sure to offer positive suggestions and comments that will help your partner improve his or her essay. Consider your partner's comments as you revise your own essay.

Additional Topics for Writing

Here are more ideas for topics for an argument essay. Before you write, be sure to refer to the seven steps in the writing process in the *Brief Writer's Handbook with Activities*, pages 156–163.

PHOTO
TOPIC: Look at the photograph on pages 112–113. Is the growth of industry more important than nature conservation? Make a decision about this issue, and write an argument essay about industry versus nature.

TOPIC 2: At what age should a person be considered an adult? Make a decision about this issue and then argue your point of view. Do not forget to include a counterargument and refutation.

TOPIC 3: Is technology (television, computers, cell phones, tablet devices, MP3 players) beneficial for children under the age of five? Should a child be allowed to have full access to technology before the age of five? Develop a thesis statement about some aspect of the age limit for technology issue and support it in your argument essay.

TOPIC 4: Should a passing score on an English achievement test be the main requirement for international students to enter a university in an English-speaking country? What are the pros and cons of this issue? Choose one side and write your essay in support of it.

TOPIC 5: The media often place heavy emphasis on the opinions and actions of celebrities, such as actors and sports stars. Should we pay attention to these opinions and actions? Are they important or not? Choose one side of this argument and write your essay in support of it.

Timed Writing

How quickly can you write in English? There are many times when you must write quickly, such as on a test. It is important to feel comfortable during those times. Timed-writing practice can make you feel better about writing quickly in English.

1. Take out a piece of paper.

2. Read the essay guidelines and the writing prompt.

3. Write a basic outline, including the thesis and your three main points.

4. Write a five-paragraph essay.

5. You have 40 minutes to write your essay.

Argument Essay Guidelines

- Be sure to include a counterargument and a refutation.

- Remember to give your essay a title.

- Double-space your essay.

- Write as legibly as possible (if you are not using a computer).

- Select an appropriate principle of organization for your topic.

- Include a short introduction (with a thesis statement), body paragraphs, and a conclusion.

- Try to give yourself a few minutes before the end of the activity to review your work. Check for spelling, verb tense, and subject–verb agreement mistakes.

What should happen to students who are caught cheating on an exam? Why?

Other Forms of Academic Writing

A photographer gets close to a 40-foot whale shark feeding on the surface near Cancun, Mexico.

OBJECTIVES To learn how to write a reaction / response essay
To learn how to answer short exam questions
To understand sentence types

*Can you write about your
reaction to a photograph
that fascinates you?*

Part I: What is a Reaction / Response Essay?

A very common type of writing task—one that appears in every academic discipline—is a **reaction** or **response** (essay). In a reaction essay, the writer is usually given a "prompt"—a visual or written stimulus—to think about and then respond to. Common prompts or stimuli for this type of writing are quotes, pieces of literature, photos, paintings, multimedia presentations, and news events. A reaction focuses on the writer's feelings, opinions, and personal observations about the particular prompt. Your task in writing a reaction essay is twofold: to briefly summarize the prompt (stimulus) and to give your personal reaction to it.

Pattern of Organization

The Introduction: A description or summary of the **thing** being reacted to.

It is very important to start with a description or summary so that the rest of your writing will make sense. In a reaction essay, your first job is to ensure that the reader has a solid understanding of what you are responding to. If you are responding to a work, such as a reading, photo, or film, make sure to mention the title and author of the work in the introduction. This paragraph also contains the **thesis statement** (usually the last sentence in this paragraph).

The Introduction	In the article *Athletes Who Have Competed in Both the Olympics and Paralympics* on Time.com, Kharunya Paramaguru focuses on the many athletes with disabilities who have competed in the Olympic Games. She provides a brief history of disabled athletes through time, their achievements, and the future trend of more disabled athletes competing in the regular Olympics. After reading the article, I was amazed by the number of disabled athletes who have actually been Olympic-class competitors and those who continue to do so.

Body (Part 1): The first reaction or response to the prompt

This includes a topic sentence and supporting details. The details can either come from the original prompt (quotes, ideas, visuals, and so on) or be original ideas and opinions.

Body (Part 1)	I was surprised to learn just how many disabled athletes have competed in the traditional Olympics (not the Paralympics) over time. Gymnasts, swimmers, and various track and field athletes are just some of the athletes who have enjoyed the competitive nature of the Olympics. In fact, when the article mentioned a young swimmer who was deaf but was nevertheless able to hear the shouting of the crowd, I was filled with awe and admiration.

Body (Part 2): The second reaction or response to the prompt

After the topic sentence, write supporting details that help to get your second point across.

Body (Reaction 2)	I was also impressed to learn that disabled athletes have been competing in the Olympic Games for over 100 years. These athletes did not wait for a special "disabled" Olympics; they just went out and competed against their peers. Sometimes, they even won—like the male gymnast in 1904 who won a gold medal even though he had a wooden leg. This was before modern prosthetics and other technological innovations.

The Conclusion: Your overall reaction to the prompt mentioned in the introduction. You may choose to evaluate whether the prompt had an overall effect or impact on you personally.

The Conclusion	In the end, I am heartened to learn about such fearless individuals who just want to compete. They are just as passionate about their sport as other professional athletes—maybe even more so. With the development of prosthetics and other devices, it may not be long until all athletes, disabled or not, can face each other in the same arena.

If you are writing a reaction essay, the organizational pattern will look something like this:

Paragraph 1	Introduction
	Summary of prompt and thesis statement
Paragraph 2	Your first reaction or response to the prompt
Paragraph 3	Your second reaction or response to the prompt
Paragraph 4	Conclusion

Writer's Note

Reaction / response writing can be as short as one paragraph and as long as 1,000 words in some cases. Your instructor will usually give you specific guidelines on how long your assignment should be.

This essay is a reaction to a particular photo. Discuss the Preview Questions with a classmate. Then read the essay and answer the questions that follow.

Preview Questions

1. Are you afraid of heights?

2. What is the highest building you have ever been in? How did you feel?

3. Study the photo below. What things come to your mind when you look at this photo? Write at least 10 things.

Essay 22

Reaction to "Old-Timer Structural Worker"

1   The photo, an image of an older construction worker on a building job, was taken in 1930 in New York City. The structure that the builder is working on still stands; it is the world famous Empire State Building, which is 102 stories tall. The black-and-white photo is a bit **grainy**, but the subject and the amazing background are clearly visible. The other tall building in the photo is the well-known Chrysler Building, another New York **landmark**. For me, this photo is a **testament** of hard work and **ingenuity**.

grainy: not smooth, granular

a landmark: sign, physical symbol

a testament: proof, demonstration

ingenuity: resourcefulness, cleverness

2   The photo portrays a man who is focused on his job. He is positioned high up in the air, yet he sits comfortably while completing his task. The old man's body language shows a keen interest in doing his job competently. Incredibly, he is not connected to harnesses or other safety equipment. The look on his face tells the story of a man with so much experience in his craft that he is not afraid of anything. What is clear is the level of comfort he portrays in the photo: comfort in his surroundings of being on an open platform over 50 stories high and comfort in his job ability.

3   The photo also represents a time of ingenuity during the early twentieth century. Looking past the man and into the horizon, one is drawn to the **countless** buildings in the distance. The fact that New York City is continuing to grow even during this period of the early 1930s is obvious in the photo. I marvel specifically at this man-made tower, which is reaching toward the sky and toward the future. The photo is a reminder of what people can create given their ingenuity, spirit, and hard work.

countless: numerous, incalculable

4   It is difficult for this photo to not **elicit** a reaction, even more than 80 years after it was taken. The visions of society and the promise of a prosperous future are ingrained in "Old-Timer Structural Worker." It is a decades-old photo that reminds us of how much we have accomplished in such a short period of time.

to elicit: bring out, obtain

Post-Reading

1. How was the introduction helpful for the reader?

2. What two main features of the picture did the writer respond to?

3. Did you have the same reaction as the writer?

4. Do you agree or disagree with the writer's responses to the photo?

Building Better Sentences: For further practice, go to Practice 22 on page 207 in Appendix 1.

ACTIVITY 2 Outlining Practice

Following is a specific outline for "Reaction to Old-Timer Structural Photo." Some of the information is missing. Reread the essay beginning on page 140 and complete the outline.

Title: _____

  I. Introduction (Paragraph 1)

    A. Summary:

      1. The photo was taken in 1930.

      2. _____

      3. The Chrysler Building is in the background.

    B. Thesis: _____

II. Body

    A. Paragraph 2 (first reaction topic sentence) The photo portrays a man who is focused on his job.

        1. His body language shows _____

               _____

               _____

        2. Safety? _____

        3. He is comfortable with _____ and _____

               _____

    B. Paragraph 3 (second reaction topic sentence) _____

           _____

        1. The buildings in the background _____

        2. _____

        3. This man-made tower _____

        4. _____

III. Conclusion (Paragraph 4)

    A. Restated thesis: _____

           _____

    B. Opinion: _____

           _____

Original Student Writing

ACTIVITY 3 **Choosing Your Prompt**

You will write a four-paragraph essay responding to a prompt or stimulus. (Remember that a paragraph usually contains four to ten sentences.) Choose one of the following five topics.

PHOTO
TOPIC: Go online and find a photo that fascinates you. Get the name of the photo (if possible), the photographer, and the website you found the photo on. Describe how this photo makes you feel. Each paragraph should include one emotion.

A wildlife farmer greets a newborn Nile crocodile in Botswana.

TOPIC 2: Choose an article that you have read recently. The article should not be more than 400 words. In the first paragraph, summarize the most important information that your reader needs to know: the name of the article, the author, and the main points of the article. Be sure to add a thesis statement that shows your intention of giving your reaction to the article.

TOPIC 3: In a newspaper, find the advice column. This is a column in many newspapers where readers seek advice on their problems. Often the problems are personal, involving family or relationships. Choose one of the problems and write a response to it. Remember to state the nature of the problem in the introduction and to include a thesis that explains your advice.

TOPIC 4: Write a reaction to a recent film you have seen. Be sure to include the name of the film, the year of release, and (preferably) the director's name. The introduction should also include a brief plot or storyline of the film so that readers who have NOT seen the film will understand your reaction. Your body paragraphs may discuss how you felt about the acting, the storyline, the graphics, character development, or cinematography. Do not write about ALL of these things: choose only two (one for each paragraph).

TOPIC 5: Watch a short documentary on TV or online (no longer than 30 minutes). Remember to begin your reaction with a summary of the program in the introductory paragraph. In the following paragraphs, write a response to what you saw. How did you feel about this program? Did you agree or disagree with it? What reaction did you have after watching it?

ACTIVITY 4 **Planning with an Outline**

Complete the outline below as a guide to help you brainstorm a more detailed plan for your reaction essay. Write in complete sentences where possible.

Topic: _____

A. Introduction (Paragraph 1)

   1. Summary of what you are reacting to:

   _____

   _____

   _____

   _____

   _____

   2. Thesis statement:

   _____

   _____

B. Reaction 1 (Paragraph 2)

   1. Topic sentence:

   _____

   _____

   2. Details and explanations:

   _____

   _____

   _____

   _____

   _____

   _____

C. Reaction 2 (Paragraph 3):

   1. Topic sentence:

   _____

   _____

2. Details and explanation:

_____

_____

_____

_____

_____

_____

D. Conclusion (Paragraph 4):

   1. Restated thesis:

_____

_____

   2. Opinion (effectiveness of prompt?):

_____

_____

_____

_____

If you need ideas for words and phrases, see the Useful Vocabulary for Better Writing on pages 185–188.

ACTIVITY 5 Peer Editing Your Outline

Exchange books with a partner and look at Activity 3. Read your partner's outline. Then use Peer Editing Sheet 9 on NGL.Cengage.com/GW4 to help you comment on your partner's outline. Use your partner's feedback to revise your outline. Make sure you have enough information to develop your supporting sentences.

ACTIVITY 6 Writing a Reaction Essay

Write a reaction essay based on your revised outline from Activity 4. Be sure to refer to the seven steps in the writing process in the *Brief Writer's Handbook with Activities* on pages 156–163.

ACTIVITY 7 Peer Editing Your Essay

Exchange papers from Activity 6 with a partner. Read your partner's essay. Then use Peer Editing Sheet 10 on NGL.Cengage.com/GW4 to help you comment on your partner's essay. Be sure to offer positive suggestions and comments that will help your partner improve his or her writing. Consider your partner's comments as you revise your own essay.

Part II: Understanding Written Exam or Essay Questions

When students take a test, they are often asked to answer "short-answer" questions. These are also called essay questions (although they are often not as long as an essay).

Here are some examples of essay questions from different academic courses:

Course	Exam Question
History	Classify the major Pacific battles of World War II in terms of number of soldiers lost on both sides.
Literature	List what you consider to be O. Henry's three best short stories. As you rank them, justify your ranking using the key components of literature (theme, plot, setting, character) presented in this course.
Biology	Explain how blood circulates through your body starting with the heart. List all of the key areas of the heart that are involved in circulation.
Economics	Discuss the recent world economic recession. Include a description of what happened and evaluate the world's major economic powers' response to the financial crisis.
Engineering	Evaluate Leonardo da Vinci's fifteenth-century model of the helicopter and compare it to today's helicopter.

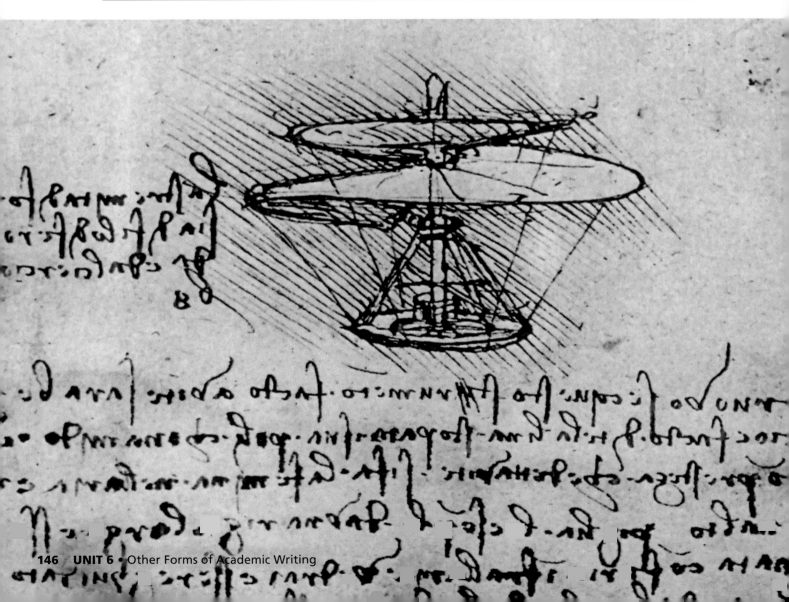

Verbs Frequently Used in Short Answer or Essay Questions

These question types require the student to produce a written answer. Following is a list of common verbs used in short-answer or essay questions. How many are you familiar with?

A. Define

Definitions call for meanings of a concept. One common definition type is the three-point definition. The three-point definition begins by explaining what general GROUP the subject is part of. Part two of the definition is an explanation of the parts or special characteristics of the object. The three-part definition ends with an example of the object.

Example Exam Question: Define "war."

Sample answer:

War is a conflict between groups of people. War includes soldiers, weapons, and attack and defense strategies. An example of a war is World War II (1939–1945).

B. Enumerate / List / Recount

These verbs ask for the writer to produce a list of items that answer the question. This answer may be introduced by a sentence (see sample answer below) that is followed by a numbered or bulleted list. Enumerations or lists do not need to be complete sentences.

Example Exam Question: **Enumerate / List / Recount** Leonardo da Vinci's most famous inventions.

Sample answer:

The following is a list of Leonardo da Vinci's most famous ideas and/or inventions:

1. The anemometer, which was used for measuring the speed of wind

2. The flying machine, a precursor to today's airplane

3. The helicopter, a machine that was modeled to fly vertically

4. The parachute, to lessen the speed of someone falling to earth

5. Scuba gear, which enabled humans to breathe under water

6. The revolving bridge, which could be quickly packed and unpacked to aid in military operations.

C. Outline

Answering a question that asks for an outline is similar to listing, but your exam answer might contain subpoints. Use the skills you already know from making essay outlines to help you answer this type of question.

Example Exam Question: Outline the benefits of aspirin on different systems of the body.

D. Summarize

When an exam question asks for a summary, you should give only the main points or facts. All details, examples, and especially personal observations should not be included.

Example Exam Question: Summarize the article "Environmental Dangers of the Twenty-First Century" in one paragraph.

E. Relate / Compare / Contrast / Distinguish / Differentiate

Some test questions will ask you to explain the relationship of something to something else. In this case, you may see these verbs. You need to explain the connections and associations of these two things, whether they are similar or different.

Example Exam Question: Relate the large numbers of immigrants to the United States in the early 1900s to the beginning of the industrial revolution.

F. Explain / Illustrate

A test question asking you to explain something or illustrate needs clarification. Very often you may use a diagram, graph, or concrete example to explain or illustrate your answer.

Example Exam Question: Illustrate the process a wind turbine uses to harness energy.

G. Evaluate / Assess / Criticize / Justify / Argue

For this type of question, you are asked to not only understand but also appraise (how good or how bad something is). This is one of the more difficult essay questions to answer because you must use critical thinking and persuasive language in your writing.

Example Exam Question: Evaluate the performance of the latest tablet computer in terms of processor size and speed.

ACTIVITY 8 **Asking and Answering Short-Answer Questions**

Choose four verbs from the box below. Write a short-answer question based on the information you have learned from this textbook. Underline the verb.

define	evaluate	illustrate	summarize
enumerate	explain	list	trace

(Your questions)

Q1: _____

_____

_____

Q2: _____

_____

_____

Q3: _____

_____

_____

Q4: _____

_____

_____

Now exchange textbooks with a classmate. Choose two of your classmate's questions and, on a separate piece of paper or on a computer, answer the questions. Try to write between 50 and 100 words in answering the essay questions.

Writer's Note

Using the Space Provided

When you are answering a short-answer question on a test, use the amount of blank (white) space on the test paper as a guide to how much information to write. Your instructors are most likely giving you a hint as to how much to include in your answer. Try to use only the allotted space and avoid writing in the margins and on the back of your exam paper.

Grammar for Writing

Understanding Sentence Types

English sentence structure includes three basic types of sentences: **simple, compound,** and **complex.** These labels indicate how the information in a sentence is organized, not how difficult the content is. Study the chart below.

Sentence Type	Parts	Examples	Notes
Simple	Subject + Verb	Alligators are common in Florida.	
Compound	Subject + Verb, (*cc) Subject + Verb	Alligators are common in Florida, but they are not easy to find in the wild.	*cc = Coordinating Conjunction: *for, and, nor, but, or, yet, so*
Complex	Independent Clause + Dependent Clause	**Whenever he gets nervous**, his hands start shaking uncontrollably.	Most complex sentences are of the **adverb clause** variety.
	Subject + Verb + **Adverb Clause**	I enjoyed **what we studied last semester**.	
	Subject + Verb + **Noun Clause**	The assignment **that was given last week** is very time consuming.	
	Subject + Verb (including **Adjective Clause**)		

ACTIVITY 9 Identifying Sentence Type

Study the 10 sentences taken from essays in this unit. Identify the sentences as simple (S), compound (C), or complex (CX).

_____ 1. The black-and-white photo is a bit grainy, but the subject and the amazing background are clearly visible.

_____ 2. The other tall building in the background is the well-known Chrysler Building, another New York landmark.

_____ 3. The structure that the builder is working on still stands.

_____ 4. For me, this photo is a testament to hard work and ingenuity.

_____ 5. The look on his face tells the story of a man with so much experience in his craft that he is not afraid of anything.

_____ 6. The photo also represents a time of ingenuity during the early twentieth century.

_____ 7. I marvel specifically at this man-made tower, which is reaching toward the sky and toward the future.

_____ 8. The visions of society and the promise of a prosperous future are ingrained in "Old-Timer Structural Worker."

_____ 9. War is a conflict between groups of people.

_____ 10. War includes soldiers, weapons, and attack and defense strategies.

Building Better Vocabulary

ACTIVITY 10 **Word Associations**

Circle the word or phrase that is most closely related to the word or phrase on the left. If necessary, use a dictionary to check the meaning of words you do not know.

	A	B
1. clarification*	better	worse
2. landmark	abstract	concrete
3. a testament	bad example	good example
4. illustrate*	ears	eyes
5. countless	few	many
6. ingenuity	dull	sharp
7. elicit	find	hide
8. enumerate	full paragraphs	list of items
9. predictions*	certainty	possibility
10. relate	connections	constructions

*Indicates words that are part of the Academic Word List. See pages 183–184 for a complete list.

ACTIVITY 11   Using Collocations

Fill in each blank with the word on the left that most naturally completes the phrase on the right. If necessary, use a dictionary to check the meaning of words you do not know.

1. from / out of   four _____ five people

2. building / testament   the photo is a _____ of

3. fast / hard   _____ work

4. by / of   your level _____ comfort

5. man-made / men-made   _____ towers

6. in / of   the promise _____ a good future

7. reaction / skyscraper   bring about a _____

8. as / by   _____ far the best movie of all time

9. between / in   a conflict _____ two groups

10. for / of   the benefits _____ education

Timed Writing

How quickly can you write in English? There are many times when you must write quickly such as on a test. It is important to feel comfortable during those times. Timed-writing practice can make you feel better about writing quickly in English.

1. Take out a piece of paper.

2. Read the essay guidelines and the writing prompt.

3. Write a basic outline, including the thesis and your three main points.

4. Write a five-paragraph essay.

5. You have 40 minutes to write your essay.

Short Answer / Essay Question Guidelines

- Review each question carefully.

- Be sure you understand the verb(s).

- Double-space your essay.

- Select an appropriate principle of organization for your topic.

- Write as legibly as possible (if you are not using a computer).

- Try to give yourself a few minutes before the end of the activity to review your work. Check for spelling, verb tense, and subject–verb agreement mistakes.

Question 1: Summarize the main points of this textbook.
(Write at least 100 words.)

Question 2: Evaluate your own academic writing skills.
(Write at least 150 words.)

Brief Writer's Handbook with Activities

Understanding the Writing Process: The Seven Steps

This section can be studied at any time during the course. You will want to refer to these seven steps many times as you write your essays.

The Assignment

Imagine that you have been given the following assignment: *Write an essay in which you discuss one aspect of vegetarianism.* What should you do first? What should you do second, third, and so on? There are many ways to write, but most good writers follow certain steps in the writing process. These steps are guidelines that are not always followed in order.

Look at this list of steps. Which ones do you regularly do? Which ones have you never done?

STEP 1: Choose a topic.

STEP 2: Brainstorm.

STEP 3: Outline.

STEP 4: Write the first draft.

STEP 5: Get feedback from a peer.

STEP 6: Revise the first draft.

STEP 7: Proofread the final draft.

Next, you will see how one student, Hamda, went through the steps to do the assignment. First, read the final essay that Hamda gave her teacher.

Essay 23

Better Living as a Vegetarian

1   The hamburger has become a worldwide cultural icon. Eating meat, especially beef, is an integral part of many diverse cultures. Studies show, however, that the consumption of large quantities of meat is a major contributing factor toward a great many deaths, including the unnecessarily high number of deaths from heart-related problems. Although it has caught on slowly in Western society, vegetarianism is a way of life that can help improve not only the quality of people's lives but also their longevity.

2   Surprising as it may sound, vegetarianism can have beneficial effects on the environment. Because demand for meat animals is so high, cattle are being raised in areas where rain forests once stood. As rain forest land is cleared in order to make room for cattle ranches, the environmental balance is upset; this imbalance could have serious consequences for humans. The article "Deforestation: The hidden cause of global warming" by Daniel Howden explains that much of the current global warming is due to depletion of the rain forests.

3   More important at an individual level is the question of how eating meat affects a person's health. Meat, unlike vegetables, can contain very large amounts of fat. Eating this fat has been connected—in some research cases—to certain kinds of cancer. In fact, *The St. Petersburg*

Times reports, "There was a statistically significant risk for . . . gastric cancer associated with consumption of all meat, red meat and processed meat" (Rao, 2006). If people cut down on the amounts of meat they ate, they would automatically be lowering their risks of disease. Furthermore, eating animal fat can lead to obesity, and obesity can cause numerous health problems. For example, obesity can cause people to slow down and their heart to have to work harder. This results in high blood pressure. Meat is also high in cholesterol, and this only adds to health problems. With so much fat consumption worldwide, it is no wonder that heart disease is a leading killer.

4   If people followed vegetarian diets, they would not only be healthier but also live longer. Eating certain kinds of vegetables, such as broccoli, brussels sprouts, and cauliflower, has been shown to reduce the chance of contracting colon cancer later in life. Vegetables do not contain the "bad" fats that meat does. Vegetables do not contain cholesterol, either. Furthermore, native inhabitants of areas of the world where people eat more vegetables than meat, notably certain areas of Central Asia, routinely live to be over one hundred.

5   Some people argue that, human nature being what it is, it is unhealthy for humans to not eat meat. These same individuals say that humans are naturally carnivores and cannot help wanting to consume a juicy piece of red meat. However, anthropologists have shown that early humans ate meat only when other foods were not abundant. Man is inherently a herbivore, not a carnivore.

6   Numerous scientific studies have shown the benefits of vegetarianism for people in general. There is a common thread for those people who switch from eating meat to consuming only vegetable products. Although the change of diet is difficult at first, most never regret their decision to become a vegetarian. They feel better, and those around them comment that they look better than ever before. As more and more people are becoming aware of the risks associated with meat consumption, they too will make the change.

Steps in the Writing Process
Step 1: Choose a Topic

For this assignment, the topic was given: Write an essay on vegetarianism. As you consider the assignment topic, you have to think about what kind of essay you may want to write. Will you list different types of vegetarian diets? Will you talk about the history of vegetarianism? Will you argue that vegetarianism is or is not better than eating animal products?

Hamda chose to write an argumentative essay about vegetarianism to try to convince readers of its benefits. The instructor had explained that this essay was to be serious in nature and have facts to back up the claims made.

Step 2: Brainstorm

The next step for Hamda was to brainstorm.

In this step, you write every idea about your topic that pops into your head. Some of these ideas will be good, and some will be bad; write them all. The main purpose of brainstorming is to write as many ideas as you can think of. If one idea looks especially good, you might circle that idea or put a check next to it. If you write an idea and you know right away that you are not going to use it, you can cross it out.

Brainstorming methods include making lists, clustering similar ideas (see Unit 2), or diagramming your thoughts (see Unit 3).

Look at Hamda's brainstorming diagram on the topic of vegetarianism.

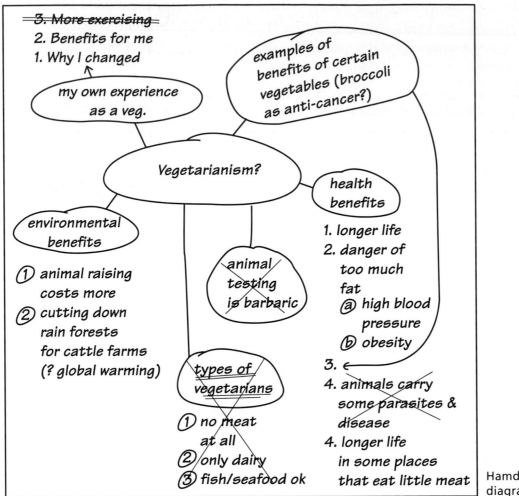

Hamda's brainstorming diagram

As you can see from the brainstorming diagram, Hamda considered many aspects of vegetarianism. Notice a few items in the diagram. As she organized her brainstorming, Hamda wrote "examples of benefits of certain vegetables" as a spoke on the wheel. Then she realized that this point would be a good number three in the list of health benefits, so she drew an arrow to show that she should move it there. Since one of Hamda's brainstorming ideas (types of vegetarians) seemed to lack supporting details and was not related to her other notes, she crossed it out.

Getting the Information

How would you get the information for this brainstorming exercise?

- You might read a book or an article about vegetarianism.

- You could spend time searching online for articles on the subject.

- You could write a short questionnaire to give to classmates asking them about their personal knowledge of vegetarian practices.

- You could also interview an expert on the topic, such as a nutritionist.

Step 3: Outline

Next, create an outline for the essay. Here is Hamda's rough outline that she wrote from her brainstorming notes.

I. Introduction

   A. Define vegetarianism

   B. List different types

   C. Thesis statement

II. Environmental benefits (Find sources to support!)

   A. Rain forests

   B. Global warming

III. Health issues (Find sources to support!)

   A. Too much fat from meat → obesity → diseases → cancer

   B. High blood pressure and heart disease

   C. Cancer-fighting properties of broccoli and cauliflower, etc.

IV. Counterargument and refutation

   A. Counterargument: Man is carnivore.

   B. Refutation

V. Conclusion

   A. Restate thesis

   B. Opinion: Life will improve.

Supporting Details

After you have chosen the main points for your essay you will need to develop some supporting details. You should include examples, reasons, explanations, definitions, or personal experiences. In some cases, such as this argumentative essay on vegetarianism, it is a good idea to include outside sources or expert opinions that back up your claims.

One common technique for generating supporting details is to ask specific questions about the topic, for example:

What is it?

What happened?

How did this happen?

What is it like or not like? Why?

Step 4: Write the First Draft

Next, Hamda wrote her first draft. As she wrote each paragraph of the essay, she paid careful attention to the language she used. She chose a formal sentence structure including a variety of sentence types. In addition, her sentences varied in length, with the average sentence containing almost 20 words. (Sentences in conversation tend to be very short; sentences in academic writing tend to be longer.) Hamda also took great care in choosing appropriate vocabulary. In addition to specific terminology, such as *obesity, blood pressure,* and *consumption,* she avoided the conversational *you* in the essay, instead referring to *people* and *individuals.*

In this step, you use information from your brainstorming session and outline to write the essay. This first draft may contain many errors, such as misspellings, incomplete ideas, and comma errors. At this point, you should not worry about correcting the errors. The main thing is to put your ideas into sentences.

You may feel that you do not know what you think about the topic yet. In this case, it may be difficult for you to write, but it is important to just write, no matter what comes out. Sometimes writing helps you think, and as soon as you form a new thought, you can write it.

Better Living as a Vegetarian

Wow — too abrupt? You don't talk about hamburgers anymore??

(Do you like hamburgers?) Eating meat, especially beef, is an ~~interesting~~ part of the

vocabulary?

daily life around the world. In addition, this high (eating) of meat is a major contributing

word choice?

causes

~~factor~~ ~~thing~~ that makes a great many deaths, including the unnecessarily high number of

deaths from heart-related problems. Vegetarianism has caught on slowly in some parts

, and it

of the world. ~~Vegetarianism~~ is a way of life that can help improve not only the quality of

people's lives but also people's longevity. → *the quality but also the length of people's lives*

This is not a topic sentence

Because demand for meat animals is (so high., Cattle) are being raised in areas where

the rainforest once stood. As rain forest land is cleared in massive amounts in order to

make room for the cattle ranches, the environmental balance is being upset. This could

For example,   *transition?*

have serious consequences for us in both the near and long term. How much of the current

global warming is due to man's disturbing the rain forest?

You need a more specific topic relating to health.

(Meat contains a high amount of fat.) Eating this fat has been connected in research

cases with certain kinds of cancer. Furthermore, eating animal fat can lead to obesity, and

obesity can cause many different kinds of diseases, for example, obesity can cause people

to slow down and their heart to have to word harder. This results in high blood pressure.

Meat is high in cholesterol, and this only adds to the health problems. With the high

consumption of animal fat by so many people, it is no wonder that heart disease is a

leading killer.

Hamda's first draft

On the other hand, eating a vegetarian diet can improve a person's health. And

necessary?

vegetables taste so good. In fact, it can even save someone's life. Eating certain kinds

of vegetables, such as broccoli, brussels sprouts, and cauliflower, has been shown to

combine sentences?

reduce the chance of having colon cancer later in life. Vegetables do not contain

the "bad" fats that meat does. Vegetables do not contain cholesterol, either. Native

inhabitants of areas of the world where mostly vegetables are consumed, notably

certain areas of the former Soviet republics, routinely live to be over one hundred.

good sentence

Although numerous scientific studies have shown the benefits of vegetarianism for people

in general, I know firsthand how my life has improved since I decided to give up meat entirely.

In 2006, I saw a TV program that discussed problems connected to animals that are raised for

food. The program showed how millions of chickens are raised in dirty, crowded conditions

not related to your topic

until they are killed. The program also talked about how diseases can be spread from cow or

pig to humans due to unsanitary conditions. Shortly after I saw this show, I decided to try life

without eating meat. Although it was difficult at first, I have never regretted my decision to

become a vegetarian. I feel better and my friends tell me that I look better than ever before.

Being a vegetarian has many benefits. Try it.

This is too short!
How about making a prediction or suggestion for the reader? The previous paragraph told how the writer became a vegetarian, so doesn't it make sense for the conclusion to say something like "I'm sure your life will be better too if you become a vegetarian"?

I like this essay. You really need to work on the conclusion.

Making Changes

As you write the first draft, you may want to add information or take some out. In some cases, your first draft may not follow your outline exactly. That is OK. Writers do not always stick with their original plan or follow the steps in the writing process in order. Sometimes they go back and forth between steps. The writing process is much more like a cycle than a line.

Reread Hamda's first draft with her teacher's comments.

First Draft Tips

Here are some things to remember about the first draft copy:

- The first draft is not the final copy. Even native speakers who are good writers do not write an essay only one time. They rewrite as many times as necessary until the essay is the best that it can be.

- It is OK for you to make notes on your drafts; you can circle words, draw connecting lines, cross out words, or write new information. Make notes to yourself about what to change, what to add, or what to reconsider.

- If you cannot think of a word or an idea as you write, leave a blank space or circle. Then go back and fill in the space later. If you write a word that you know is not the right one, circle or underline it so you can fill in the right word later. Do not stop writing. When people read your draft, they can see these areas you are having trouble with and offer comments that may help.

- Do not be afraid to throw some sentences away if they do not sound right. Just as a good housekeeper throws away unnecessary things from the house, a good writer throws out unnecessary or wrong words or sentences.

The handwriting in the first draft is usually not neat. Sometimes it is so messy that only the writer can read it! Use a word-processing program, if possible, to make writing and revising easier.

Step 5: Get Feedback from a Peer

Hamda used Peer Editing Sheet 8 to get feedback on her essay draft. Peer editing is important in the writing process. You do not always see your own mistakes or places where information is missing because you are too close to the essay that you created. Ask someone to read your draft and give you feedback about your writing. Choose someone that you trust and feel comfortable with. While some people feel uneasy about peer editing, the result is almost always a better essay. Remember to be polite when you edit another student's paper.

Step 6: Revise the First Draft

This step consists of three parts:

1. React to the comments on the peer editing sheet.
2. Reread the essay and make changes.
3. Rewrite the essay one more time.

Step 7: Proofread the Final Draft

Most of the hard work is over now. In this step, the writer pretends to be a brand-new reader who has never seen the essay before. Proofread your essay for grammar, punctuation, and spelling errors and to see if the sentences flow smoothly.

Read Hamda's final paper again on pages 156–157.

Of course, the very last step is to turn the paper in to your teacher and hope that you get a good grade!

Writer's Note

Proofreading

One good way to proofread your essay is to set it aside for several hours or a day or two. The next time you read your essay, your head will be clearer and you will be more likely to see any problems. In fact, you will read the composition as another person would.

Editing Your Writing

While you must be comfortable writing quickly, you also need to be comfortable with improving your work. Writing an assignment is never a one-step process. For even the most gifted writers, it is often a multiple-step process. When you were completing your assignments in this book, you probably made some changes to your work to make it better. However, you may not have fixed all of the errors. The paper that you turned in to your teacher is called a first draft, which is sometimes referred to as a rough draft.

A first draft can often be improved. One way to improve an essay is to ask a classmate, friend, or teacher to read it and make suggestions. Your reader may discover that one of your paragraphs is missing a topic sentence, that you have made grammar mistakes, or that your essay needs better vocabulary choices. You may not always like or agree with the comments from a reader, but being open to changes will make you a better writer.

This section will help you become more familiar with how to identify and correct errors in your writing.

Step 1

Below is a student's first draft for a timed writing. The writing prompt for this assignment was "For most people, quitting a job is a very difficult decision. Why do people quit their jobs?" As you read the first draft, look for areas that need improvement and write your comments. For example, does the writer use the correct verb tenses? Is the punctuation correct? Is the vocabulary suitable for the intended audience? Does the essay have an appropriate hook?

There Are Many Reasons Why People Quit Their Jobs

Joann quit her high-paying job last week. She had had enough of her coworkers' abuse. Every day they would make fun of her and talk about her behind her back. Joann's work environment was too stressful, so she quit. Many employees quit their jobs. In fact, there are numerous reasons for this phenomenon.

First, the job does not fit the worker. Job seekers may accept a job without considering their skills. Is especially true when the economy is slowing and jobs are hard to find. The workers may try their best to change themselves depending on the work. However, at some point they realize that they are not cut out in this line of work and end up quitting. This lack of understanding or ability make people feel uncomfortable in their jobs. So they begin to look for other work.

Another reason people quit their jobs is the money. Why do people work in the first place? They work in order to make money. If employees are underpaid, he cannot earn enough to support himself or his family. The notion of working, earning a decent salary, and enjoy life is no longer possible. In this case, low-paid workers have no choice but to quit their jobs and search for a better-paying position.

Perhaps the biggest situation that leads people to quit their jobs is personality conflicts. It is really difficult for an employee to wake up every morning, knowing that they will be spending the next eight or nine hours in a dysfunctional environment. The problem can be with bosses or coworkers but the result is the same. Imagine working for a discriminate boss or colleagues which spread rumors. The stress levels increases until that employee cannot stand the idea of going to work. The employee quits his or her job in the hope of finding a more calm atmosphere somewhere else.

Work should not be a form of punishment. For those people who have problems with not feeling comfortable on the job, not getting paid enough, and not respected, it *does* feel like punishment. As a result, they quit and continue their search for a job that will give them a sense of pride, safety, and friends.

Step 2

Read the teacher's comments on the first draft of "There Are Many Reasons Why People Quit Their Jobs." Are these the same things that you noticed?

The title should NOT be a complete sentence.

There Are Many Reasons Why People Quit Their Jobs

Consider changing your hook/introduction. The introduction here is already explaining one of the reasons for quitting a job. This information should be in the body of the essay. Suggestion: Use a "historical" hook describing how people were more connected to their jobs in the past than they are now.

Joann quit her high-paying job last week. She had had enough of her coworkers' abuse. Every

day they would make fun of her and talk about her behind her back. Joann's work environment

was too stressful, so she quit. Many employees quit their jobs. In fact, there are numerous reasons

for this phenomenon.

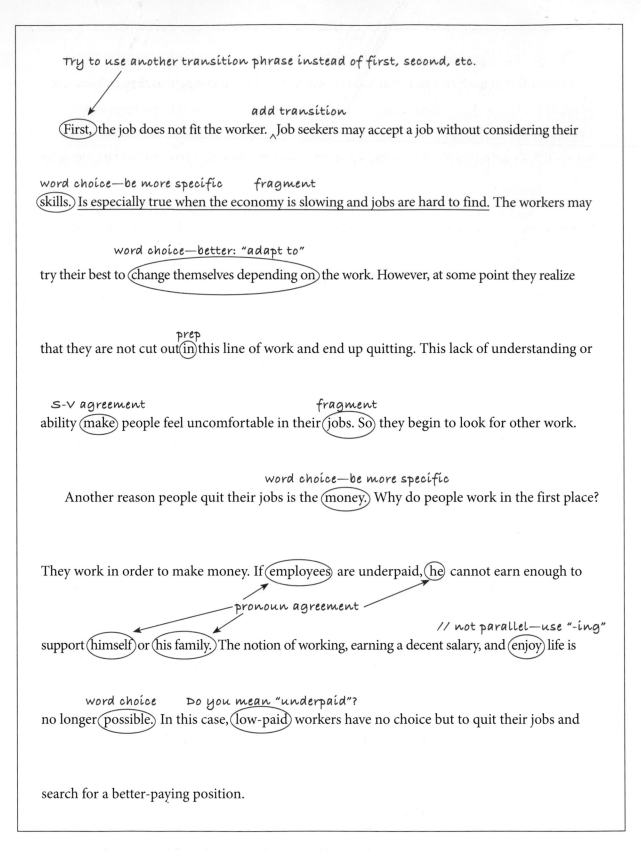

Try to use another transition phrase instead of first, second, etc.

add transition

(First,) the job does not fit the worker. ∧ Job seekers may accept a job without considering their

word choice—be more specific *fragment*

(skills.) <u>Is especially true when the economy is slowing and jobs are hard to find.</u> The workers may

word choice—better: "adapt to"

try their best to (change themselves depending on) the work. However, at some point they realize

prep

that they are not cut out (in) this line of work and end up quitting. This lack of understanding or

S-V agreement *fragment*

ability (make) people feel uncomfortable in their (jobs. So) they begin to look for other work.

word choice—be more specific

Another reason people quit their jobs is the (money.) Why do people work in the first place?

They work in order to make money. If (employees) are underpaid, (he) cannot earn enough to

pronoun agreement

// not parallel—use "-ing"

support (himself) or (his family.) The notion of working, earning a decent salary, and (enjoy) life is

word choice *Do you mean "underpaid"?*

no longer (possible.) In this case, (low-paid) workers have no choice but to quit their jobs and

search for a better-paying position.

word choice—too vague

Perhaps the (biggest) situation that leads people to quit their jobs is personality conflicts. It is

word choice—avoid using "really"   *pronoun agreement*

(really) difficult for an employee to wake up every morning, knowing that (they) will be spending

add another descriptive word here   *word choice—too vague*

the next eight or nine hours in a dysfunctional ^ environment. The (problem) can be with bosses

punc. (add comma)   *word choice*

or coworkers but the result is the same. Imagine working for a (discriminate) boss or colleagues

word form   *S-V agreement*   *write it out—better: "can no longer"*

(which) spread rumors. The stress levels (increases) until that employee (can't) stand the idea of

add transition   *word choice—better: "serene"*

going to work. ^ The employee quits his or her job in the hope of finding a more (calm) atmosphere

somewhere else.

thought of as   *word choice*

Work should not be ^ a form of punishment. For those people who (have problems) with not

// not parallel—use "-ing"

feeling comfortable on the job, not getting paid enough, and (not respected,) it *does* feel like

punishment. As a result, they quit and continue their search for a job that will give them a

word choice—better: "camaraderie"

sense of pride, safety, and (friends.)

Step 3

Now read the second draft of this essay. How is it the same as the first draft? How is it different? Did the writer fix all the sentence mistakes?

Two Weeks' Notice

A generation ago, it was common for workers to stay at their place of employment for years and years. When it was time for these employees to retire, companies would offer a generous pension package and, sometimes, a token of appreciation, such as a watch, keychain, or other trinket. Oh, how times have changed. Nowadays, people—especially younger workers—jump from job to job like bees fly from flower to flower to pollinate. Some observers might say that today's workforce is not as serious as yesterday's. This is too simple an explanation, however. In today's society, fueled by globalization, recession, and other challenges, people quit their jobs for a number of valid reasons.

One reason for quitting a job is that the job does not fit the worker. In other words, job seekers may accept a job without considering their aptitude for it. This is especially true when the economy is slowing and jobs are hard to find. The workers may try their best to adapt themselves to the work. However, at some point they realize that they are not cut out for this line of work and end up quitting. This lack of understanding or ability makes people feel uncomfortable in their jobs, so they begin to look for other work.

Another reason people quit their jobs is the salary. Why do people work in the first place? They work in order to make money. If employees are underpaid, they cannot earn enough to support themselves or their families. The notion of working, earning a decent salary, and enjoying life is no longer viable. In this case, underpaid workers have no choice but to quit their jobs and search for a better-paying position.

Perhaps the most discouraging situation that leads people to quit their jobs is personality conflicts. It is extremely difficult for an employee to wake up every morning knowing that he or she will be spending the next eight or nine hours in a dysfunctional and often destructive environment. The discord can be with bosses or coworkers, but the result is the same. Imagine working for a bigoted boss or colleagues who spread rumors. The stress levels increase until that employee can no longer stand the idea of going to work. In the end, the employee quits his or her job with the hope of finding a more serene atmosphere somewhere else.

Work should not be thought of as a form of punishment. For those people who struggle with not feeling comfortable on the job, not getting paid enough, and not being respected, it *does* feel like punishment. As a result, they quit and continue their search for a job that will give them a sense of pride, safety, and camaraderie.

Sentence Types

English sentence structure includes three basic types of sentences: simple, compound, and complex. These labels indicate how the information in a sentence is organized, not how difficult the content is.

Simple Sentences

1. Simple sentences usually contain one subject and one verb.

       S   V
       [Kids] love television.

      V   S   V
      Does [this] sound like a normal routine?

2. Sometimes simple sentences can contain more than one subject or verb.

              S   V
     [Brazil and the United States] are large countries.

       S   V   V
     [Brazil] lies in South America and has a large population.

      S   V   V
     [We] traveled throughout Brazil and ended our trip in Argentina.

Compound Sentences

Compound sentences are usually made up of two simple sentences (independent clauses). Compound sentences need a coordinating conjunction (connector) to combine the two sentences. The coordinating conjunctions include:

     for   and   nor   but   or   yet   so

Many writers remember these conjunctions with the acronym *FANBOYS*. Each letter represents one conjunction: *F = for, A = and, N = nor, B = but, O = or, Y = yet,* and *S = so.*

Remember that a comma is always used before a coordinating conjunction that separates the two independent clauses.

             S   V   S   V
for   [Meagan] studied hard, **for** [she] wanted to pass the test.

             S   V   S   V
and   [Meagan] studied hard, **and** [her classmates] studied, too.

             S   V   V   S   V
nor   [Meagan] did not study hard, **nor** did [she] pass the test.

             S   V   S   V
but   [Meagan] studied hard, **but** [her brother] did not study at all.

             S   V   S   V
or   [Meagan] studied hard, **or** [she] would have failed the test.

             S   V   S   V
yet   [Meagan] studied hard, **yet** [she] was not happy with her grade.

             S   V   S   V
so   [Meagan] studied hard, **so** [the test] was easy for her.

Study the following examples of compound sentences. Draw a box around each subject, underline each verb, and circle each coordinating conjunction.

1. Brazil was colonized by Europeans, and its culture has been greatly influenced by this fact.

2. This was my first visit to the international section of the airport, and nothing was familiar.

3. Many people today are overweight, and being overweight has been connected to some kinds of cancer.

4. Barriers fell, markets opened, and people rejoiced in the streets because they anticipated a new life full of opportunities and freedom to make their own choices.

5. Should public school students make their own individual decisions about clothing, or should all students wear uniforms?

6. This question has been asked many times, but people are not in agreement about the ultimate punishment.

Complex Sentences

Like compound sentences, complex sentences are made up of two parts. Complex sentences, however, contain one independent clause and, at least, one dependent clause. In most complex sentences, the dependent clause is an adverb clause.

Complex Sentences (with Adverb Clauses)

Adverb clauses begin with subordinating conjunctions, which include the following:

while   although   after   because   if   before

Study the examples below. The adverb clauses are underlined, and the subordinating conjunctions are boldfaced.

The hurricane struck **while** we were at the mall.

After the president gave his speech, he answered most of the reporters' questions.

NOTE: A more complete list of subordinating conjunctions can be found in the Connectors section of the *Brief Writer's Handbook with Activities*, pages 180–181.

Unlike coordinating conjunctions, which join two independent clauses but are not part of either clause, subordinating conjunctions are actually part of the dependent clause.

Joe played tennis   **after** Vicky watched TV.

independent clause   dependent clause

The subordinating conjunction *after* does not connect the clauses *Joe played tennis* and *Vicky watched TV*; *after is* grammatically part of *Vicky watched TV.*

Remember that dependent clauses must be attached to an independent clause. They cannot stand alone as a sentence. If they are not attached to another sentence, they are called fragments, or incomplete sentences. Fragments are incomplete ideas, and they cause confusion for the reader. In a complex sentence, both clauses are needed to make a complete idea so the reader can understand what you mean. Look at these examples:

Fragment: After Vicky watched TV

Complete Sentence: Joe played tennis after Vicky watched TV.

                           or

Complete Sentence: After Vicky watched TV, she went to bed.

Study the following examples of complex sentences from the essays in this book. Draw a box around each subject, underline each verb, and circle each subordinating conjunction.

1. While the Northeast is experiencing snowstorms, cities like Miami, Florida, can have temperatures over 80 degrees Fahrenheit.

2. Although Brazil and the United States are unique countries, there are remarkable similarities in their size, ethnic diversity, and personal values.

3. Another bus arrived at the terminal, and the passengers stepped off carrying all sorts of luggage.

4. While it is true that everyone makes a blunder from time to time, some people do not have the courage to admit their errors because they fear blame.

5. Because almost every area has a community college, students who opt to go to a community college first can continue to be near their families for two more years.

Additional Grammar Activities

The three example essays in this section feature different grammatical errors. Each paragraph highlights one kind of error. In each case, read the entire essay before you complete the activities.

Before you complete Activities 1–5, read the whole essay first. Then go back and complete each activity.

ACTIVITY 1 Verb Forms

Read the paragraph and decide whether the five underlined verbs are correct. If not, draw a line through the verb and write the correct form above the verb.

Essay 24

A Simple Recipe

1   "When in Rome, do as the Romans do" may <u>sound</u> ridiculous, but this proverb <u>offer</u> an important suggestion. If you travel to other countries, especially to a country that is very different from your own, you should <u>keeping</u> this saying in mind. For example, Japan has unique customs that <u>is</u> not found in any other country. If you <u>traveled</u> to Japan, you should find out about Japanese customs, taboos, and people beforehand.

ACTIVITY 2 Verb Forms

Read this paragraph carefully. Then write the correct form of the verbs in parentheses.

2   One custom is that you should (take) _____ off your shoes before (enter) _____ someone's house. In Japan, the floor must always be kept clean because usually people (sit) _____, eat a meal, or even (sleep) _____ on the floor. Another custom

is giving gifts. The Japanese often (give) _____ a small gift
to people who have (do) _____ favors for them. Usually this
token of gratitude (give) _____ in July and December to keep
harmonious relations with the receiver. When you (give) _____
someone such a gift, you should make some form of apology about it. For
example, many Japanese will say, "This is just a small gift that I have for you."
In addition, it is not polite to open a gift immediately. The receiver usually
(wait) _____ until the giver has left so the giver will not be
embarrassed if the gift (turn) _____ out to be defective or
displeasing.

ACTIVITY 3 Connectors

Read the paragraph carefully. Then fill in the blanks with one of these connectors:

    because   in addition   even if   for example   first   but

3   _____, it is important to know about Japanese
taboos. All cultures have certain actions that are considered socially
unacceptable. _____ something is acceptable in one culture,
it can easily be taboo in another culture. _____, chopsticks
are used in many cultures, _____ there are two taboos about
chopsticks etiquette in Japan. _____, you should never stand
the chopsticks upright in your bowl of rice. _____ standing
chopsticks upright is done at a funeral ceremony, this action is associated
with death. Second, you must never pass food from one pair of chopsticks
to another. Again, this is related to burial rites in Japan.

ACTIVITY 4 Articles

There are 14 blanks in this paragraph. Read the paragraph and write the articles *a, an,* or *the* to
complete the sentences. Some blanks do not require articles.

4   Third, it is important to know that Japanese people have
_____ different cultural values. One of _____
important differences in _____ cultural values is
_____ Japanese desire to maintain _____
harmony at all costs. People try to avoid causing any kind of dispute.
If there is _____ problem, both sides are expected to
compromise in order to avoid an argument. People are expected to
restrain their emotions and put _____ goal of compromise
above their individual wishes. Related to this is _____
concept of patience. Japanese put _____ great deal of

_____ value on _____ patience. Patience
also contributes to maintaining _____ good relations with
_____ everyone and avoiding _____ disputes.

Read this paragraph and write the correct preposition in each blank. Choose from these prepositions:
into, in, to, about, with, of, and *around.* You may use them more than once.

5 _____ conclusion, if you want to get along well
_____ the Japanese and avoid uncomfortable situations
when you go _____ Japan, it is important to take
_____ account the features _____ Japanese
culture that have been discussed here. Although it may be hard to
understand Japanese customs because they are different, knowing
_____ them can help you adjust to life in Japan. If you face
an unfamiliar or difficult situation when you are _____
Japan, you should do what the people _____ you do. In other
words, "When _____ Japan, do as the Japanese do."

Before you complete Activities 6–12, read the whole essay. Then go back and complete each activity.

ACTIVITY 6 Verb Forms

Read this paragraph carefully. Then write the correct form of the verbs in parentheses.

Dangers of Corporal Punishment

1 What should parents do when their five-year-old child says
a bad word even though the child knows it is wrong? What should a
teacher (do) _____ when a student in the second grade
(call) _____ the teacher a name? When my parents (be)
_____ children forty or fifty years ago, the answer to these
questions was quite clear. The adult would spank the child immediately.
Corporal punishment (be) _____ quite common then. When
I was a child, I (be) _____ in a class in which the teacher got
angry at a boy who kept (talk) _____ after she told him to
be quiet. The teacher then (shout) _____ at the boy and, in

front of all of us, (slap) _____ his face. My classmates and I were shocked. Even after twenty years, I still remember that incident quite clearly. If the teacher's purpose (be) _____ to (teach) _____ us to (be) _____ quiet, she did not (succeed) _____. However, if her purpose was to create an oppressive mood in the class, she succeeded. Because corporal punishment (be) _____ an ineffective and cruel method of discipline, it should never be (use) _____ under any circumstances.

ACTIVITY 7 Prepositions

Read this paragraph carefully. Write the correct preposition in each blank. Use these prepositions: *in, of,* and *for.*

2   Supporters _____ corporal punishment claim that physical discipline is necessary _____ developing a child's sense _____ personal responsibility. Justice Lewis Powell, a former U.S. Supreme Court justice, has even said that paddling children who misbehave has been an acceptable method _____ promoting good behavior and responsibility _____ school children for a long time. Some people worry that stopping corporal punishment in schools could result _____ a decline _____ school achievement. However, just because a student stops misbehaving does not mean that he or she suddenly has a better sense _____ personal responsibility or correct behavior.

ACTIVITY 8 Articles

Read the paragraph and write the articles *a, an,* or *the* to complete the sentences. Some blanks do not require articles.

3   Corporal punishment is _____ ineffective way to punish _____ child because it may stop a behavior for a while, but it will not necessarily have _____ long-term effect. Thus, if an adult inflicts _____ mild form of _____ corporal punishment that hurts the child very little or not at all, it will not get rid of the bad behavior. Moreover, because corporal punishment works only temporarily, it will have to be repeated whenever the child misbehaves. It may then become _____ standard response to any misbehavior. This can lead to _____ frequent and more severe spanking, which may result in _____ abuse.

ACTIVITY 9 Comma Splices

Read this paragraph carefully and find the two comma splices. Correct them in one of two ways:
(1) change the comma to a period and make two sentences or (2) add a connector after the comma.

4   A negative effect of corporal punishment in school is that it makes some students feel aggressive toward parents, teachers, and fellow students. In my opinion, children regard corporal punishment as a form of teacher aggression that makes them feel helpless. Therefore, students may get frustrated if corporal punishment is used frequently. Furthermore, it increases disruptive behavior that can become more aggressive, this leads to school violence and bullying of fellow students. Supporters of corporal punishment believe that it is necessary to maintain a good learning environment, it is unfortunate that the opposite result often happens. The learning environment actually becomes less effective when there is aggressive behavior.

ACTIVITY 10 Verb Forms

Read the paragraph and decide whether the underlined verbs are correct. If not, draw a line through the verb and write the correct form above it.

5   Last, corporal punishment may <u>result</u> in antisocial behavior later in life because it teaches children that adults <u>condone</u> violence as a solution to problems. Children who are <u>spank</u> learn that it is acceptable for a stronger person <u>using</u> violence against a weaker person. The concept of "might makes right" is <u>forced</u> upon them at a very early age. Furthermore, this concept teaches a lesson not only to those who are spanked but also to those who <u>witness</u> it. Studies of prisoners and delinquents <u>shows</u> that nearly 100 percent of the violent inmates at San Quentin and 64 percent of juvenile delinquents <u>was</u> victims of seriously abusive punishment during childhood. If serious punishment <u>causes</u> antisocial behavior, perhaps even milder punishment also <u>contribute</u> to violence. Research at the University of New Hampshire <u>will find</u> that children who were spanked between the ages of three and five <u>showed</u> higher levels of antisocial behavior when they <u>were observed</u> just two and four years later. This behavior included higher levels of beating family members, <u>hitting</u> fellow students, and defying parents. It is ironic that the behaviors for which teachers <u>punishing</u> students often get worse as a result of the spanking.

ACTIVITY 11 Editing for Errors

There are seven errors in this paragraph. They are in word forms (two), articles (one), sentence fragments (one), verb tense (one), and subject-verb agreement (two). Mark these errors and write corrections.

6   For punishment to be effective, it must produce a great behavioral change, result in behavior that is permanent, and produce minimal side effects. However, none of these changes is a result of corporal punishment. Therefore, we should consider alternatives to corporal punishment. Because discipline is necessary to educate children. One of the alternatives are to emphasize students' positive behaviors. Some research shows that reward, praise, and self-esteem is the most powerful motivators for the learning. Other alternatives are to hold conferences with students to help them plan acceptable behave or to use school staff, such as psychologists and counselors. It is important to build better interpersonal relations between teachers and students. In addition to these alternatives, instruction that reaches all students, such as detention, in-school suspension, and Saturday school, is available to discipline and punishment unruly students, too. Alternatives to corporal punishment taught children to be self-disciplined rather than to be cooperative only because of fear.

ACTIVITY 12 Editing for Errors

There are seven errors in this paragraph. They are in word forms (one), articles (three), sentence fragments (one), comma splices (one), and subject-verb agreement (one). Mark these errors and write the corrections.

7   In the conclusion, teachers should not use corporal punishment because it is ineffective in disciplining students and may have long-term negative effects on students. Moreover, teachers should not forget that love and understanding must be part of any kind of discipline. Discipline and love is not opposites, punishment must involve letting the children know that what they do is wrong and why punishment is necessary. Teachers should not just beat student with the hopeful that he will understand. It is important to maintain discipline without inflicting physical pain on students. Therefore, teachers should use effective and more humane alternatives. In order to bring about permanent behavioral changes.

Before you complete Activities 13–18, read the whole essay. Then go back and complete each activity.

ACTIVITY 13 Articles

Read the paragraph and write the articles *a, an,* or *the* to complete the sentences. Some blanks do not require articles.

Washington and Lincoln

1   Perhaps no other names from _____ American history are better known than the names of George Washington and Abraham Lincoln. Both of these presidents made valuable contributions to _____ United States during their presidency. In fact, one could argue that _____ America would not be _____ same country that it is today if either of these two leaders had not been involved in _____ American politics. However, it is interesting to note that although both leaders made _____ significant contributions to _____ country, they lived in _____ quite different times and served in _____ very different ways.

ACTIVITY 14 Verb Forms

Read this paragraph carefully. Then write the correct form of the verbs in parentheses.

2   Everyone (know) _____ that George Washington was the first president of the United States. What most people do not (appreciate) _____ (be) _____ that Washington (be) _____ a clever military leader. He served the country in the early days of the Revolution by (help) _____ to change the colonial volunteers from ragged farmers into effective soldiers. Without Washington's bravery and military strategy, it is doubtful that the colonies could have (beat) _____ the British. Thus, without Washington, the colonies might never even have (become) _____ the United States of America.

ACTIVITY 15 Prepositions

Read this paragraph and write the correct preposition in each blank. Choose from these prepositions: *from, in, to, with, for, between,* and *of.* You may use them more than once.

3   Abraham Lincoln was the sixteenth president _____ the United States. He was elected president _____ 1860 during a controversial and heated period of American history. As more states applied _____ membership in the growing country, the issue _____ slavery kept surfacing. There was an unstable balance _____ slave states and free states. Each time another state was added _____ the Union, the balance of power shifted. Lincoln was _____ a free state, and many _____ the slave state leaders viewed Lincoln as an enemy of their cause _____ expand slavery. _____ the end, no compromise could be reached, and the slave states seceded _____ the United States in order to form their own independent country. Hostilities grew, and _____ 1861 the Civil War, or the War _____ the States as it is sometimes called, broke out. During the next four years, the Civil War ravaged the country. By the end of the war in 1865, the American countryside was _____ shambles, but the Union was once again intact. Through his military and political decisions, Lincoln is credited _____ saving the country _____ self-destruction.

ACTIVITY 16 Editing for Errors

There are eight errors in this paragraph. They are in word forms (one), articles (two), modals (one), verb tense (two), and subject-verb agreement (two). Mark these errors and write corrections.

4   Washington and Lincoln was similarly in several ways. Both men are U.S. presidents. Both men served the United States during extremely difficult times. For Washington, the question is whether the United States would be able to maintain its independence from Britain. The United States was certainly very fragile nation at that time. For Lincoln, the question were really not so different. Would the United States to be able to survive during what was one of darkest periods of American history?

ACTIVITY 17 Sentence Fragments

After you read this paragraph, find the three sentence fragments. Correct the fragments by (1) changing the punctuation and creating one complete sentence or (2) adding new words to make the fragment a complete sentence.

5   There were also several differences between Washington and Lincoln. Washington came from a wealthy aristocratic background. He had several years of schooling. Lincoln came from a poor background, and he had very little schooling. Another difference between the two involved their military roles. Washington was a general. He was a military leader. Became president. Lincoln never served in the military. He was a lawyer who early on became a politician. When he became president, he took on the role of commander in chief, as all U.S. presidents do. Despite his lack of military background or training. Lincoln made several strategic decisions that enabled the U.S. military leaders to win the Civil War. Finally, Washington served for two terms and therefore had eight years to accomplish his policies. Lincoln, on the other hand, was assassinated. While in office and was not able to finish some of the things that he wanted for the country.

ACTIVITY 18 Editing for Errors

There are seven errors in this paragraph. They are in articles (two), verb tense (one), inappropriate words (one), word forms (one), number (singular and plural) (one), and subject-verb agreement (one). Mark these errors and make corrections.

6   The names George Washington and Abraham Lincoln is known even to people who have never been to the United States. Both of these patriots gave large part of their lives to help America make what it is today though they served the country in very different ways in complete different time in the American history. Although they were gone, their legacies and contributions continue to have an impact on our lives.

Connectors

Using connectors will help your ideas flow. Remember that when connectors occur at the beginning of a sentence, they are often followed by a comma.

Purpose	Coordinating Conjunctions (connect independent clauses)	Subordinating Conjunctions (begin dependent clauses)	Transitions (usually precede independent clauses)
Examples			For example, To illustrate, Specifically, In particular,
Information	and		In addition, Moreover, Furthermore,
Comparison			Similarly, Likewise, In the same way,
Contrast	but	while, although	In contrast, However, On the other hand, Conversely, Instead,
Refutation			On the contrary,
Concession	yet	although though even though it may appear that	Nevertheless, Even so, Admittedly, Despite this,
Emphasis			In fact, Actually,
Clarification			In other words, In simpler words, More simply,
Reason/Cause	for	because since	
Result	so	so so that	As a result, As a consequence, Consequently, Therefore, Thus,
Time Relationships		after as soon as before when while until whenever as	Afterward, First, Second, Next, Then Finally, Subsequently, Meanwhile, In the meantime,
Condition		if even if unless provided that when	

Purpose	Coordinating Conjunctions (connect independent clauses)	Subordinating Conjunctions (begin dependent clauses)	Transitions (usually precede independent clauses)
Purpose		so that in order that	
Choice	or		
Conclusion			In conclusion, To summarize, As we have seen, In brief, In closing, To sum up, Finally,

Citations and Plagiarism

When writing a paragraph or an essay, writers should use their own words for the most part. Sometimes, however, writers want to use ideas that they have read in a book, an article, on a website, or even heard in a speech. It can make the paragraph or essay more interesting, more factual, or more relevant to the reader. For example, if a writer is working on a paragraph about a recent election, he or she may want to use a quotation from a famous politician. In this case, the writer must indicate that the words are not his or her own, but that they came from someone else. Indicating that a writer's words are not original is called **citing**. In academic writing, it is necessary for a writer to cite all sources of information that are not original.

If the information does not come from the writer's head, it must be cited.

Writers who do not—whether intentionally or unintentionally—give credit to the original author are **plagiarizing**, or stealing, someone else's words. **This is academic theft, and most institutions take this very seriously.**

To avoid plagiarism, it is important to use quotes or a paraphrase which includes an in-text citation, and add a reference or bibliography at the end of your writing.

Using Quotes

Quotations are used when a writer wants to keep the source's exact words. See the examples.

✓ The original reference is the source.

✓ The reference itself is the bibliographical reference.

✓ Use quotation marks " " for original words.

✓ The following verbs are often used to introduce quotes.

describes	points out	states
argues	finds	predicts
claims	insists	reports

Examples: Here are three different examples of quoting a sentence from a text.

Original: There is absolutely no empirical evidence – quantitative or qualitative – to support the familiar notion that monolingual dictionaries are better than bilingual dictionaries for understanding and learning L2.

Quote 1: According to Folse (2004), "There is absolutely no empirical evidence – quantitative or qualitative – to support the familiar notion that monolingual dictionaries are better than bilingual dictionaries for understanding and learning L2."

Quote 2: And while instructors continue to push for monolingual dictionaries, "there is absolutely no empirical evidence – quantitative or qualitative – to support the familiar notion that monolingual dictionaries are better than bilingual dictionaries for understanding and learning L2." (Folse, 2004).

Quote 3: As Folse points out, "There is absolutely no empirical evidence – quantitative or qualitative – to support the familiar notion that monolingual dictionaries are better than bilingual dictionaries for understanding and learning L2" (2004).

Reference/Bibliography

Folse, Keith. *Vocabulary Myths: Applying Second Language Research to Classroom Teaching*. Ann Arbor: University of Michigan Press, 2004.

Paraphrasing

Sometimes writers want to paraphrase or summarize outside information. In this case, the same rules still hold true. **If it is not from the writer's head, it must be cited.**

Original: Every year, the town of Vinci, Italy, receives as many as 500,000 visitors—people coming in search of its most famous son, Leonardo.

Paraphrase: Although a small town, Vinci is visited by many tourists because it is the birthplace of Leonardo da Vinci (Herrick, 2009).

Original: This quiet, unimposing hill town is relatively unchanged from the time of Leonardo.

Paraphrase: Herrick (2009) explains that even after 500 years, the town of Vinci has remained pretty much the same.

Reference/Bibliography

Herrick, T. (2009, January 1). Vinci: A Visit to Leonardo's Home Town. *Offbeat Travel*. Retrieved May 1, 2013, from www.offbeattravel.com/vinci-italy-davinci-home.html

Bibliography

At the end of your paragraph or essay, you must list the sources you used. There are several formats (APA, Chicago, or MLA) for documenting your sources. Always check with your instructor before turning in a paper or essay. This bibliography usually includes the author(s), the publication name, the city, the publisher, the publication year, the media type, and the page number or website.

Here are some guidelines for referencing different works:

Source	Include	Example
Book	Name of author, title of book, publication city: publisher, and year of publication.	Folse, Keith. *Vocabulary Myths: Applying Second Language Research to Classroom Teaching.* Ann Arbor: University of Michigan Press, 2004.
Online Article	Name of author (if there is one), title of article, name of Web page, date of publication (if there is one), name of website, Accessed date from URL	"Great Website Design," *Website Design Basics*, http://www.websitedesignbasics.com, Accessed June 26, 2013
Website	Name of Web page, date, name of Web site. Accessed date, URL	"Global Warming 101." *Union of Concerned Scientists*. Accessed December 14, 2012, http://www.ucsusa.org/global_warming/global_warming_101/
Newspaper	Name of author, title of article, name of newspaper, section date, and page numbers.	Smith, Steven, "What To Do in Case of Emergencies." *USA Today*, December 13, 2008, 2–3.
Speech/ Interview	Name of author, title of speech or interview, place or course, and date.	Vestri, Elena. Understanding Logical Fallacies. Lecture, ENGL 102, Khalifa University, Abu Dhabi. Feb. 21, 2013.

Academic Word List

Averil Coxhead (2000)

The following words are on the Academic Word List (AWL). The AWL is a list of the 570 highest-frequency academic word families that regularly appear in academic texts. The AWL was compiled by researcher Averil Coxhead based on her analysis of a 3.5 million word corpus.

abandon	automate	confer	derive	ethnic
abstract	available	confine	design	evaluate
academy	aware	confirm	despite	eventual
access	behalf	conflict	detect	evident
accommodate	benefit	conform	deviate	evolve
accompany	bias	consent	device	exceed
accumulate	bond	consequent	devote	exclude
accurate	brief	considerable	differentiate	exhibit
achieve	bulk	consist	dimension	expand
acknowledge	capable	constant	diminish	expert
acquire	capacity	constitute	discrete	explicit
adapt	category	constrain	discriminate	exploit
adequate	cease	construct	displace	export
adjacent	challenge	consult	display	expose
adjust	channel	consume	dispose	external
administrate	chapter	contact	distinct	extract
adult	chart	contemporary	distort	facilitate
advocate	chemical	context	distribute	factor
affect	circumstance	contract	diverse	feature
aggregate	cite	contradict	document	federal
aid	civil	contrary	domain	fee
albeit	clarify	contrast	domestic	file
allocate	classic	contribute	dominate	final
alter	clause	controversy	draft	finance
alternative	code	convene	drama	finite
ambiguous	coherent	converse	duration	flexible
amend	coincide	convert	dynamic	fluctuate
analogy	collapse	convince	economy	focus
analyze	colleague	cooperate	edit	format
annual	commence	coordinate	element	formula
anticipate	comment	core	eliminate	forthcoming
apparent	commission	corporate	emerge	found
append	commit	correspond	emphasis	foundation
appreciate	commodity	couple	empirical	framework
approach	communicate	create	enable	function
appropriate	community	credit	encounter	fund
approximate	compatible	criteria	energy	fundamental
arbitrary	compensate	crucial	enforce	furthermore
area	compile	culture	enhance	gender
aspect	complement	currency	enormous	generate
assemble	complex	cycle	ensure	generation
assess	component	data	entity	globe
assign	compound	debate	environment	goal
assist	comprehensive	decade	equate	grade
assume	comprise	decline	equip	grant
assure	compute	deduce	equivalent	guarantee
attach	conceive	define	erode	guideline
attain	concentrate	definite	error	hence
attitude	concept	demonstrate	establish	hierarchy
attribute	conclude	denote	estate	highlight
author	concurrent	deny	estimate	hypothesis
authority	conduct	depress	ethic	identical

identify	lecture	paradigm	register	subsequent
ideology	legal	paragraph	regulate	subsidy
ignorant	legislate	parallel	reinforce	substitute
illustrate	levy	parameter	reject	successor
image	liberal	participate	relax	sufficient
immigrate	license	partner	release	sum
impact	likewise	passive	relevant	summary
implement	link	perceive	reluctance	supplement
implicate	locate	percent	rely	survey
implicit	logic	period	remove	survive
imply	maintain	persist	require	suspend
impose	major	perspective	research	sustain
incentive	manipulate	phase	reside	symbol
incidence	manual	phenomenon	resolve	tape
incline	margin	philosophy	resource	target
income	mature	physical	respond	task
incorporate	maximize	plus	restore	team
index	mechanism	policy	restrain	technical
indicate	media	portion	restrict	technique
individual	mediate	pose	retain	technology
induce	medical	positive	reveal	temporary
inevitable	medium	potential	revenue	tense
infer	mental	practitioner	reverse	terminate
infrastructure	method	precede	revise	text
inherent	migrate	precise	revolution	theme
inhibit	military	predict	rigid	theory
initial	minimal	predominant	role	thereby
initiate	minimize	preliminary	route	thesis
injure	minimum	presume	scenario	topic
innovate	ministry	previous	schedule	trace
input	minor	primary	scheme	tradition
insert	mode	prime	scope	transfer
insight	modify	principal	section	transform
inspect	monitor	principle	sector	transit
instance	motive	prior	secure	transmit
institute	mutual	priority	seek	transport
instruct	negate	proceed	select	trend
integral	network	process	sequence	trigger
integrate	neutral	professional	series	ultimate
integrity	nevertheless	prohibit	sex	undergo
intelligent	nonetheless	project	shift	underlie
intense	norm	promote	significant	undertake
interact	normal	proportion	similar	uniform
intermediate	notion	prospect	simulate	unify
internal	notwithstanding	protocol	site	unique
interpret	nuclear	psychology	so-called	utilize
interval	objective	publication	sole	valid
intervene	obtain	publish	somewhat	vary
intrinsic	obvious	purchase	source	vehicle
invest	occupy	pursue	specific	version
investigate	occur	qualitative	specify	via
invoke	odd	quote	sphere	violate
involve	offset	radical	stable	virtual
isolate	ongoing	random	statistic	visible
issue	option	range	status	vision
item	orient	ratio	straightforward	visual
job	outcome	rational	strategy	volume
journal	output	react	stress	voluntary
justify	overall	recover	structure	welfare
label	overlap	refine	style	whereas
labor	overseas	regime	submit	whereby
layer	panel	region	subordinate	widespread

Useful Vocabulary for Better Writing

Try these useful words and phrases as you write your essays. Many of these are found in the *Great Writing 4: Great Essays* models, and they can make your writing sound more academic, natural, and fluent.

Comparing

Words and Phrases	Examples
NOUN *is* COMPARATIVE ADJECTIVE *than* NOUN.	New York *is larger than* Rhode Island.
S + V + COMPARATIVE ADVERB *than* NOUN.	The cats ran *faster than* the dogs.
S + V. *In comparison*, S + V.	Canada has provinces. *In comparison*, Brazil has states.
Although NOUN *and* NOUN *are similar in* NOUN, …	*Although* France and Spain *are similar in* size, they are different in many ways.
Upon close inspection, S + V.	*Upon close inspection*, teachers in both schools discovered their students progressed *faster* when using games.
Compared to…	*Compared to* these roses, those roses last a long time.
NOUN *and* NOUN *are surprisingly similar.*	Brazil *and* the United States *are surprisingly similar.*
The same…	Brazil has states. *The same* can be said about Mexico.
Like NOUN, NOUN *also…*	*Like* Brazil, Mexico *also* has states.
Compared to…	*Compared to* U.S. history, Chinese history is complicated.
Both NOUN *and* NOUN…	*Both* dictatorships *and* oligarchies exemplify non-democratic ideologies.
Also, S + V. / *Likewise*, S + V.	The economies in South America seem to be thriving. *Likewise*, some Asian markets are doing very well these days.
Similarly, S + V. / *Similar to* S + V.	The economies in South America seem to be thriving. *Similarly*, some Asian markets are doing very well these days.

Contrasting

Words and Phrases	Examples
S + V. *In contrast*, S + V.	Algeria is a very large country. *In contrast*, the U.A.E. is very small.
Contrasted with / *In contrast to* NOUN	*In contrast to* soda, water is a better alternative.
Although / *Even though* / *Though…*	*Although* Spain and France are similar in size, they are different in many other ways.
Unlike NOUN, NOUN…	*Unlike* Spain, France borders eight countries.
However, S + V.	Canada has provinces. *However*, Brazil has states.
One the one hand, S + V. *On the other hand*, S + V.	*On the one hand*, Maggie loved to travel. *On the other hand*, she hated to be away from her home.
S + V, *yet* S + V.	People know that eating sweets is not good for their health, *yet* they continue to eat more sugar and fat than ever before.
NOUN *and* NOUN *are surprisingly different.*	Finland *and* Iceland *are surprisingly different.*

Telling a Story/Narrating

Words and Phrases	Examples
When I was NOUN *I* ADJ, *I would* VERB.	*When I was* a child, *I would* go fishing every weekend.
I had never felt so ADJ *in my life.*	*I had never felt so* anxious *in my life.*
I never would have thought that…	*I never would have thought that* I could win the competition.
Then the most amazing thing happened.	I thought my bag was gone forever. *Then the most amazing thing happened.*
Whenever I think back to that time, …	*Whenever I think back to* my childhood, I am moved by my grandparents' love for me.
I will never forget NOUN	*I will never forget* my wedding day.
I can still remember NOUN / *I will always remember* NOUN	*I can still remember* the day I started my first job.
NOUN *was the best / worst day of my life.*	The day I caught that fish *was the best day of my life.*
Every time S + V, S + V.	*Every time* I used that computer, I had a problem.
This was my first NOUN	*This was my first* time traveling alone.

Showing Cause and Effect

Words and Phrases	Examples
Because S + V / *Because of* S + V	*Because of* the traffic problems, it is easy to see why the city is building a new tunnel.
NOUN *can trigger* NOUN NOUN *can cause* NOUN	An earthquake *can trigger* tidal waves and *can cause* massive destruction.
Due to NOUN	*Due to* the economic sanctions, the unemployment rate skyrocketed.
On account of NOUN / *As a result of* NOUN / *Because of* NOUN	*On account of* the economic sanctions, the unemployment rate skyrocketed.
Therefore, NOUN / *As a result,* NOUN / *For this reason,* NOUN / *Consequently,* NOUN	Markets fell. *Therefore,* millions of people lost their life savings.
NOUN *will bring about* NOUN	The use of the Internet *will bring about a* change in education.
NOUN *has had a positive / negative effect on* NOUN	Computer technology *has had both positive and negative effects* on society.
The correlation… is clear / evident.	*The correlation* between junk food and obesity *is clear.*

Stating an Opinion

Words and Phrases	Examples
Without a doubt, doing NOUN *is* ADJECTIVE *idea / method / decision / way.*	*Without a doubt,* walking to work each day *is* an excellent *way* to lose weight.
Personally, I believe / think / feel / agree / disagree / suppose that NOUN	*Personally, I believe that* using electronic devices on a plane should be allowed.
Doing NOUN *should not be allowed.*	Texting in class *should not be allowed.*
In my opinion / view / experience, NOUN	*In my opinion,* talking on a cell phone in a movie theater is extremely rude.
For this reason, NOUN / *That is why I think* NOUN	*For this reason,* voters should not pass this law.

There are many benefits / advantages to NOUN.	*There are many benefits to* swimming every day.
There are many drawbacks / disadvantages to NOUN.	*There are many drawbacks to* eating meals at a restaurant.
I *am convinced that* S + V.	I *am convinced that* nuclear energy is safe and energy efficient.
NOUN *should be required / mandatory.*	Art education *should be required* of all high school students.
I *prefer* NOUN *to* NOUN.	I *prefer* rugby *to* football.
To me, banning / prohibiting NOUN *makes sense.*	*To me, banning* cell phones while driving *makes perfect sense.*
For all of these important reasons, S + V.	*For all of these important reasons,* cell phones in schools should be banned.
Based on NOUN, S + V.	*Based on* the facts presented, high-fat foods should be banned from the cafeteria.

Arguing and Persuading

Words and Phrases	Examples
It is important to remember S + V	*It is important to remember that* school uniforms would only be worn during school hours.
According to a recent survey, S + V	*According to a recent survey,* 85 percent of high school students felt they had too much homework.
Even more important, S + V	*Even more important,* statistics show the positive effects that school uniforms have on behavior.
Despite this, S + V	*Despite this,* many people remain opposed to school uniforms.
S *must / should / ought to*	Researchers *must* stop unethical animal testing.
For these reasons, S + V	*For these reasons,* public schools should require uniforms.
Obviously, S + V	*Obviously,* citizens will get used to this new law.
Without a doubt, S + V	*Without a doubt,* students ought to learn a foreign language.
I *agree that* S + V; *however,* S + V	I *agree that* a college degree is important; *however,* getting a practical technical license can also be very useful.

Giving a Counterargument

Words and Phrases	Examples
Proponents / Opponents may say S + V	*Opponents* of uniforms *may say* that students who wear uniforms cannot express their individuality.
On the surface this might seem logical / smart / correct; however, S + V	*On the surface this might seem logical; however,* it is not an affordable solution.
S + V; *however, this is not the case.*	The students could attend classes in the evening; *however, this is not the case.*
One could argue that S + V, *but* S + V	*One could argue that* working for a small company is very exciting, *but* it can also be more stressful than a job in a large company.
It would be wrong to say that S + V	*It would be wrong to say that* nuclear energy is 100 percent safe.
Some people believe that S + V	*Some people believe that* nuclear energy is the way of the future.

Upon further investigation, S + V	*Upon further investigation,* one begins to see problems with this line of thinking.
However, I cannot agree with this idea.	Some people think logging should be banned. *However, I cannot agree with this idea.*
Some people may say (one opinion), *but I* (opposite opinion.)	*Some people may say that* working from home is lonely, *but I* believe that working from home is easy, productive, and rewarding.
While NOUN *has its merits,* NOUN…	*While* working outside the home *has its merits,* working from home has many more benefits.
Although it is true that…, S + V	*Although it is true that* taking online classes can be convenient, it is difficult for many students to stay on task.

Reacting/Responding

Words and Phrases	Examples
TITLE *by* AUTHOR *is a / an* …	*Harry Potter and the Goblet of Fire by* J.K. Rowling *is an* entertaining book to read.
My first reaction to the prompt / news / article was / is NOUN	*My first reaction to the article was* fear.
When I read / look at / think about NOUN, *I was amazed / shocked / surprised* …	*When I read* the article, *I was surprised* to learn of his athletic ability.

Appendices

Appendix 1

Building Better Sentences

Being a good writer involves many skills, such as being able to use correct grammar, vary vocabulary usage, and state ideas concisely. Some student writers like to keep their sentences simple because they feel that if they create longer and more complicated sentences, they are more likely to make mistakes. However, writing short, choppy sentences one after the other is not considered appropriate in academic writing. Study these examples:

The time was yesterday.

It was afternoon.

There was a storm.

The storm was strong.

The movement of the storm was quick.

The storm moved towards the coast.

The coast was in North Carolina.

Notice that every sentence has an important piece of information. A good writer would not write all these sentences separately. Instead, the most important information from each sentence can be used to create one longer, coherent sentence.

Read the sentences again below and notice that the important information has been circled.

The time was (yesterday.)

It was (afternoon.)

There was a (storm.)

The storm was (strong.)

The (movement) of the storm was (quick.)

The storm moved towards the (coast.)

The coast was in (North Carolina.)

Here are some strategies for taking the circled information and creating a new sentence.

1. Create time phrases to introduce or end a sentence: yesterday + afternoon
2. Find the key noun: storm
3. Find key adjectives: strong
4. Create noun phrases: a strong + storm
5. Change word forms: movement = move; quick = quickly
   moved + quickly
6. Create prepositional phrases: towards the coast
   towards the coast (of North Carolina)
   or
   towards the North Carolina coast

Now read this improved, longer sentence:

Yesterday afternoon, a strong storm moved quickly towards the North Carolina coast.

Here are some more strategies for building better sentences:

7. Use coordinating conjunctions (*and, but, or, nor, yet, for, so*) to connect two sets of ideas.

8. Use subordinating conjunctions, such as *after, while, since,* and *because,* to connect related ideas.

9. Use clauses with relative pronouns, such as *who, which, that,* and *whose,* to describe or define a noun or noun phrase.

10. Use pronouns to refer to previously mentioned information.

11. Use possessive adjectives and pronouns, such as *my, her, his, ours,* and *theirs.*

    Study the following example.

    (Susan) (went) somewhere. That place was (the mall.) Susan wanted to (buy new shoes.) The shoes were for (Susan's mother.)

    Now read the improved, longer sentence:

    Susan went to the mall because she wanted to buy new shoes for her mother.

Practices

Follow these steps for each practice:

Step 1: Read the sentences. Circle the most important information in each sentence.

Step 2: Write an original sentence from the information you circled. Use the strategies listed on page 190 and this page. Remember that there is more than one way to combine sentences.

Practice 1 Unit 1

A. 1. There is (another chore.)
   2. The chore is in the (household.)
   3. (Many people dislike) this chore.
   4. The chore is (washing dishes.)

   Another household chore that many people dislike is washing dishes.

B. 1. The bathroom is full of germs.
   2. Because of this, a wiping is not enough.
   3. The wiping is quick.
   4. The wiping is of the surfaces.

   _____

   _____

C. 1. The task is so unpleasant.
   2. The task is cleaning the bathroom.
   3. Some people wear gloves when they attempt it.
   4. The gloves are made of rubber.

   _____

   _____

D. 1. Maintaining a house means doing something.

    2. The "something" is chores.

    3. There is a wide variety of chores.

    4. The chores are unpleasant.

_____

_____

Practice 2 Unit 1

A. 1. I saw the letter.

    2. The letter was from someone.

    3. As soon as I saw it, I did something.

    4. I started sweating.

_____

_____

B. 1. I turned.

    2. I saw her.

    3. She had a lovely smile.

_____

_____

C. 1. My mouth was so dry.

    2. I could barely do something.

    3. I answered her.

_____

_____

D. 1. The letter was in my hand.

    2. I jumped off the sofa.

    3. I ran to my mother.

    4. I showed my mother.

_____

_____

Practice 3 Unit 1

A. 1. The situation is just the opposite.

    2. The situation is in a town.

3. The situation is often.

4. The town is small.

_____

_____

B. 1. It is rare to find things there.

2. The things are museums or restaurants.

3. The restaurants are exotic.

_____

_____

C. 1. Finally, people might be disappointed.

2. These people enjoy shopping.

3. They are disappointed in the number of stores.

4. The number of stores is small.

_____

_____

D. 1. Other differences exist, too.

2. The differences are important.

3. None of the differences makes one place better than the other.

_____

_____

Practice 4 Unit 1

A. 1. However, eating foods can increase a person's chance for some kinds of disease.

2. The foods are fatty.

3. The disease is cancer.

_____

_____

B. 1. The diet must be in conjunction with exercise.

2. The diet is improved.

3. The exercise is regular.

_____

_____

C. 1. People had jobs.

    2. The jobs required more labor.

    3. The labor was physical.

    4. All this information is additional.

_____

_____

D. 1. Sunburn damages the skin.

    2. Repeated damage may lead to cancer.

    3. The cancer is of the skin.

    4. This can happen later in life.

_____

_____

Practice 5 Unit 1

A. 1. A diploma is not the end of many people's education.

    2. The diploma is from high school.

    3. This happens these days.

_____

_____

B. 1. Making this choice requires a great deal of thought.

    2. This choice is difficult.

    3. The thought is careful.

_____

_____

C. 1. Going to a university requires high school graduates to live far from home.

    2. This happens often.

    3. The students have graduated recently.

    4. Many of the graduates are reluctant to live far from home.

_____

_____

D. 1. A campus offers a large variety of sports events and social activities.

    2. The campus is at a university.

3. Students can easily become distracted.

4. The distractions are related to their studies.

_____

_____

Practice 6 Unit 1

A. 1. People retire from their jobs.

   2. This happens when they reach a certain age.

   3. The age is 65.

   4. This happens traditionally.

_____

_____

B. 1. There is a belief.

   2. This belief is nothing but a misconception.

   3. This belief is common.

   4. The belief is that a person's mind slows down after a certain age.

_____

_____

C. 1. They are worried about something.

   2. If older workers are allowed to continue in their jobs, something will happen.

   3. There will not be enough openings.

   4. The openings are for younger people.

_____

_____

D. 1. In conclusion, the age of retirement should be decided by an individual's need.

   2. The need is economic.

   3. It should also be decided by an individual's health status.

   4. It should also be decided by an individual's personal preference.

_____

_____

Practice 7 Unit 1

A. 1. Coaches are responsible for training their athletes.

    2. Coaches are responsible for focusing on each individual.

    3. The individual has strengths.

    4. The individual has weaknesses.

_____

_____

B. 1. Athletes tend to be very competitive.

    2. This competitiveness leads to arguments.

    3. This happens often.

    4. This happens in practice and during games.

_____

_____

C. 1. Managers know that teamwork is vital.

    2. It is vital to productivity.

    3. They are trained to make sure that the workplace runs smoothly.

_____

_____

D. 1. They write up reports to keep the owners informed about information.

    2. The information is about who is doing well.

    3. The information is about who is injured.

    4. The information is about who is not performing up to par.

_____

_____

Practice 8 Unit 2

A. 1. This was my first visit to the airport.

    2. It was the international section.

    3. Nothing was familiar.

_____

_____

B. 1. I tried to ask a businessman for help.

    2. He was passing.

3. All my words came out wrong.

_____

_____

C. 1. Tears formed in my eyes.

   2. I saw the lobby.

   3. It was deserted.

   4. I realized that I would miss my airplane.

_____

_____

D. 1. He smiled.

   2. It was a kind smile.

   3. He took me by the hand.

   4. He led me down a long hallway.

_____

_____

Practice 9 Unit 2

A. 1. As a result, I did something.

   2. I got rid of this e-mail.

   3. The e-mail was superstitious.

   4. I did it with one click of the mouse

   5. The click was quick.

_____

_____

B. 1. I woke up the next morning.

   2. I was surprised to find something.

   3. I had overslept.

   4. I would be late for work.

_____

_____

C. 1. I arrived at work.

   2. I found a note.

   3. It was on my desk.

4. It was from my boss.

_____

_____

D. 1. I put on my reading glasses.

  2. I began scrolling through my list.

  3. The list was of my e-mail friends.

_____

_____

Practice 10 Unit 2

A. 1. My idol is a person.

  2. I have known this person my entire life.

_____

_____

B. 1. As usual, we were woken up.

  2. A sound woke us up.

  3. The sound was of our sister.

  4. She was playing the piano.

_____

_____

C. 1. It was obvious.

  2. This was a day.

  3. The day was important.

  4. It was important for everyone.

_____

_____

D. 1. Claudio meant something.

  2. It was time.

  3. The time was for me.

  4. I needed to take on a role in the family.

  5. The role was bigger.

_____

_____

Practice 11 Unit 2

A. 1. My father asked me to turn on the car.

   2. He proceeded to guide me.

   3. He guided me into reverse.

_____

_____

B. 1. My father had me drive around.

   2. I drove around the same block.

   3. This happened again and again.

_____

_____

C. 1. I was flying.

   2. I was in the sedan.

   3. It was old.

_____

_____

D. 1. All the information leaked out.

   2. I had learned this information in the previous weeks.

   3. The leak was out of my brain.

_____

_____

Practice 12 Unit 3

A. 1. Brazil's weather varies greatly.

   2. This is because of the large size of Brazil.

   3. These variations occur from one area to another.

_____

_____

B. 1. Brazil was colonized.

   2. The colonists were Europeans.

   3. Brazil's culture has been influenced by this fact.

   4. The influence has been great.

_____

_____

C. 1. There is a mixture of cultures.

   2. There is a mixture of customs.

   3. The mixture has worked to form something.

   4. The result is ethnically rich cultures in both countries.

_____

_____

D. 1. Citizens believe that they have the right.

   2. They can do whatever they desire.

   3. They can be whatever they desire.

   4. This right exists as long as they do not hurt others.

_____

_____

Practice 13 Unit 3

A. 1. Still, shoppers need to know something.

   2. They are computer shoppers.

   3. They are today's shoppers.

   4. They need to know what their options are.

_____

_____

B. 1. A buyer needs to reach a decision.

   2. He or she can compare these two computer types.

   3. He or she compares them in terms of their overall cost.

   4. He or she compares their convenience.

   5. He or she compares their style.

_____

_____

C. 1. Choosing between a model is a decision.

   2. The decision is personal.

   3. The decision is for the consumer.

   4. The model types are desktop and laptop.

_____

_____

D. 1. It can seem like a task now.

   2. The task is daunting.

   3. It will become more and more difficult.

   4. This is certain.

   5. New species of computers come on the market.

_____

_____

Practice 14 Unit 3

A. 1. The film previews are finished.

   2. The movie theater is quiet.

   3. Everyone waits for something.

   4. They wait for the feature film to begin.

_____

_____

B. 1. There is a toddler.

   2. The toddler is sitting in the movie theater.

   3. He is uncomfortable.

   4. Perhaps he is unhappy.

_____

_____

C. 1. A child does something.

   2. It is something careless like break a glass.

   3. Lenient parents will not become angry.

   4. They will not scream.

_____

_____

D. 1. Most fall somewhere in the middle.

   2. It depends on the child.

   3. It depends on the environment.

   4. It depends on the particular situation.

_____

_____

Practice 15 Unit 4

A. 1. The celebrated story of Pinocchio teaches us the importance of something.

    2. He begins life as a puppet.

    3. It is important to tell the truth.

_____

_____

B. 1. There is another reason people lie.

    2. People lie to get out of situations.

    3. They do not want to be in these situations.

    4. They cannot manage these situations.

_____

_____

C. 1. In this situation, lying can prevent some things.

    2. The lying is protective.

    3. The lying can prevent harm.

    4. The lying can prevent disaster.

_____

_____

D. 1. People lie for many reasons.

    2. The reasons are good.

    3. The reasons are bad.

_____

_____

Practice 16 Unit 4

A. 1. Tensions between two groups were high.

    2. The two groups were the Western countries and the Soviet Union.

    3. The world felt a potential danger.

    4. The danger was of a disastrous conflict.

_____

_____

B. 1. One of the most obvious changes has been the shift.

    2. Changes occurred in the post-communist world.

3. The shift is to a market economy.

_____

_____

C. 1. These republics are in a process.

   2. This process is current.

   3. They are shaping their identities.

   4. Their identities are their own.

   5. Their identities are independent.

_____

_____

D. 1. They do not want to be repatriated to lands.

   2. The lands are distant.

   3. There are lands such as North Korea or China.

_____

_____

Practice 17 Unit 4

A. 1. Mr. Stevenson has just come home from somewhere.

   2. He came from work.

   3. He had a terribly tiring day there.

_____

_____

B. 1. People use television for some reasons.

   2. They use television to relax.

   3. They use television to forget about troubles.

   4. The troubles occur daily.

_____

_____

C. 1. There is another problem with TV watching.

   2. It may cause children to have difficulty distinguishing between some things.

   3. They do not know what is real.

   4. They do not know what is not real.

_____

_____

D. 1. Television has changed over the years.

   2. It now includes more and more programs.

   3. These programs are inappropriate for children.

_____

_____

Practice 18 Unit 4

A. 1. Studying is not for everyone.

   2. The studying happens abroad.

   3. This is certain.

_____

_____

B. 1. One effect of studying abroad is a student's greater understanding.

   2. The effect is important.

   3. The understanding is of an educational system.

   4. The system is different.

_____

_____

C. 1. The host country's language is the same.

   2. There are many experiences.

   3. The experiences are cultural.

   4. The student will have these experiences.

_____

_____

D. 1. As a result, the student should remember something.

   2. He must represent his country.

   3. He must represent his culture.

   4. The representation must be in the best possible light.

_____

_____

Practice 19 Unit 5

A. 1. Most people believe in the right to express their opinion.

   2. The opinion is their own.

   3. They do not have fear.

   4. The fear is punishment.

_____

_____

B. 1. Uniforms give students a message.

   2. School is a special place.

   3. It is a place used for learning.

_____

_____

C. 1. Students' standards of living differ.

   2. The differences are great.

   3. The differences occur from family to family.

   4. Some people are well-off.

   5. Others are not well-off.

_____

_____

D. 1. Studies show something about students when they wear uniforms.

   2. Students learn better.

   3. Students act more responsibly.

_____

_____

Practice 20 Unit 5

A. 1. It was the year.

   2. Diana, Princess of Wales was killed in that year.

   3. She was killed in a car accident.

   4. The accident was horrific.

_____

_____

B. 1. Many people decided something.

   2. Diana, Princess of Wales was the victim.

   3. She was a victim of reporters.

   4. The reporters were overly aggressive.

_____

_____

C. 1. The debate continues.

   2. The topic of the debate is celebrity privacy.

   3. Almost everyone has an opinion.

   4. It seems that way.

_____

_____

D. 1. Celebrities are often role models.

   2. They need to be prepared for the cameras.

   3. The cameras belong to the paparazzi.

   4. They need to be prepared at all times.

_____

_____

Practice 21 Unit 5

A. 1. The EU has one concern.

   2. The concern is major.

   3. It is the death penalty.

_____

_____

B. 1. There is a second reason.

   2. It allows for capital punishment.

   3. The reason is financial.

_____

_____

C. 1. These criminals do not actively improve society.

   2. Society must provide them free things.

   3. Society provides housing.

4. Society provides food.

_____

_____

D. 1. There are many reasons.

   2. The reasons are good.

   3. The reasons are to allow for the death penalty.

_____

_____

Practice 22 Unit 6

A. 1. The photo was taken in 1930.

   2. The photo was taken in New York City.

   3. The photo is an image of an older construction worker.

   4. The worker is on a building job.

_____

_____

B. 1. There is another building in the photo.

   2. The building is tall.

   3. It is the Chrysler Building.

   4. The Chrysler Building is well known.

   5. It is another landmark.

   6. It is in New York City.

_____

_____

C. 1. He is not connected to harnesses.

   2. He is not connected to other safety equipment.

   3. This is incredible.

_____

_____

D. 1. It is a decades-old photo. The photo reminds us of something.

   2. We have accomplished so much.

   3. This has happened in such a short period of time.

_____

_____

Appendix 2

Peer Editing Sheet Sample

This is an example of the Peer Editing Sheets available for *Great Writing 4: Great Essays*. For units 1–6, the Peer Editing Sheets can be downloaded at NGL.Cengage.com/GW4.

Unit 1: Narrative Essay Outline

Writer: _____ Date: _____

Peer Editor: _____ Topic: _____

1. Is the hook interesting? _____ If not, how could it be made more interesting? _____

_____

2. How many paragraphs are going to be in the essay? _____

3. What action or event does each topic sentence show?

   Paragraph 1: _____

   Paragraph 2: _____

   Paragraph 3: _____

   Paragraph 4: _____

   Paragraph 5: _____

4. Is there a good ending to the action of the story? _____ If not, can you suggest a change to

   the ending? _____

5. What kind of ending will the story have—a moral, prediction, or revelation? _____

6. Do you think this essay will have enough information? _____ Does the story leave out

   anything important? Write suggestions here _____

7. The best part of the outline is _____

8. Questions I still have about the outline: _____

Index